FOLLOW ME

My Story About Poverty In America
1960-2021

LEON SWARTS, Ed.D

Charleston, SC
www.PalmettoPublishing.com

FOLLOW ME

Paperback ISBN: 978-1-63837-388-9
eBook ISBN: 978-1-68515-383-0

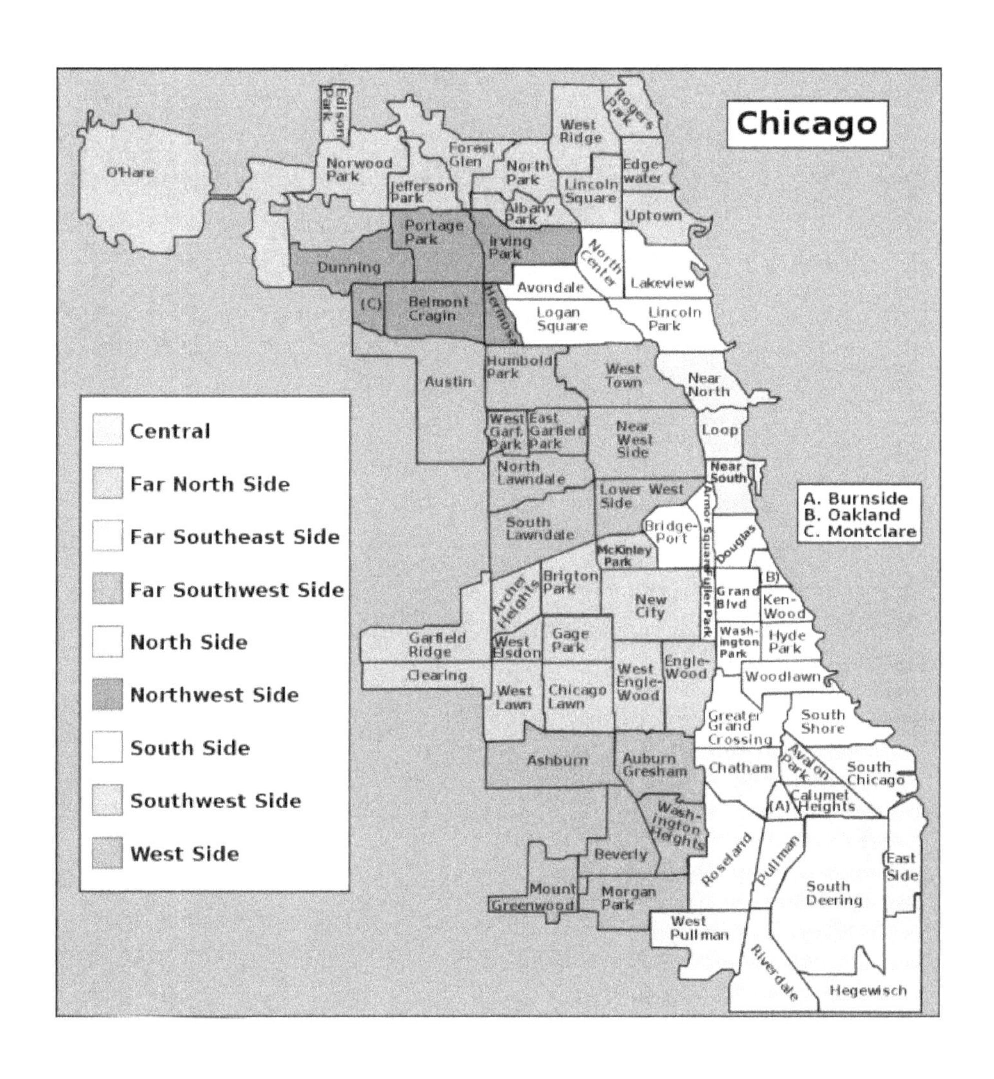

Seventy-seven areas - 2021

DEDICATION AND ACKNOWLEDGEMENT

This novel is dedicated to all the educators, counselors, social workers and psychologists who have devoted their lives and careers to help poor families and children in small and large cities across America.

Because of their work, tens of thousands Americans who live in poverty are able to benefit from their support and resources.

"Hats off to them!"

OUTLINE

PREFACE

The book is about a ten year old boy growing up in Chicago. His father dies and his family loses their home. They end up living in a project on the south side. The main character is faced with situational poverty and struggles to overcome its obstacles. As the main character matures he realizes that poverty is a huge American problem. He uses his education and career to help but learns there are political realities that perpetuate poverty. The story outcome is positive but the reality is poverty continues to exist from generation to generation.

The book offers an inspirational and educational perspective. The main character develops counselling and psychological skills to help the poor. The strategies and practices he uses are demonstrated in real life situations. Children and family case studies and situational scenarios are developed and described as examples to help the poor. The book offers data driven research as a means to assess the needs of poor children and families.

A by-product of the book is its educational component. The content offers strategies and practices for college and university students to consider as they seek degrees as counselors, social workers and psychologists.

The main goal of the book is to explore poverty in America during a sixty-year period. The research and data suggest that poverty is directly related to political policies and ideology. The solutions to reducing poverty are numerous but worthy of all efforts.

PROLOGUE

My eyes opened slowly and the sunlight hit my face like a hot poker. I realized immediately that it was a bright and sparkling spring afternoon. As I focused my eyes, I felt a warm breeze filter through the front porch opening. Birds chirped and flew freely among the tall oak trees.

The front door squeaked and slammed against its frame! The loud bang fully awakened every nerve, muscle and tendon in my body. I looked up from my porch rocking chair and heard my wife's high-pitched voice. "Did you fall asleep?" Latisha asked. "No, although I may have dozed off for a couple of minutes," Louis replied. "More like a couple of hours," Latisha responded. "Did you take your medicine?" she asked. "No," Louis replied. "Do I have to remind you every day. You can take your pills before we eat supper," Latisha responded. "Okay," I spoke.

I loved Latisha dearly but often felt she was a little overprotective and a bit nagging. She was two years younger than me. I had just turned seventy a couple of months ago. We had been married for twenty-five years and met while working at Chicago's Family Services Center. We had fostered two children and now enjoyed our much deserved retirement. We cherished our house, the neighborhood we lived in, and our beloved front porch. We lived on a beautiful tree lined and well-kept street on the south side of Chicago's Hyde Park.

Latisha had aged gracefully. She was healthy, energetic and enjoyed an active lifestyle despite an early life setback. I, however, was less fortunate. I had inherited my family's heart disease and take daily blood pressure and cholesterol medication.

Latisha sat next to me, as I gently rocked in my favorite porch chair. I looked at her as she calmly read a magazine. I told her that I had dream about telling my life story to a young boy who lived in the neighborhood. "Did you see him?" I asked. "No," she replied. "I think he was about ten years old, and I had seen him riding his skateboard past our house several times. It was probably just a dream," Latisha responded. "Are you sure you didn't hear me talking to anyone?" he asked. "I am certain," she spoke.

"I guess you're right," I responded. "Let's go in and get ready for supper and don't forget to take your medicine," she said. I got up from my rocking chair reluctantly and followed Latisha into the house. The door squeaked and slammed against its frame.

After supper, Latisha and I washed the dishes and tidied the kitchen. She asked, "Would you like to watch TV?" "Okay," I responded. "Would you enjoy the story about the inner-city family that struggled with short-term situational poverty, but eventually through hard work was able to find a better life?" she asked. "Okay with me," I spoke.

While we watched TV, my mind wandered back to the young boy's porch visit. Whether it was a dream or just my imagination; I couldn't get the thought out of my head. I looked at Latisha, tears streaming down her cheeks and realized she was fully absorbed in the family poverty story.

Rather than bother her, I began to think about writing a story about my life. Latisha looked up from the TV, turned it off and wiped the tears from her eyes with a Kleenex. "Did you enjoy the story?" I asked. She responded, "Yes, even though I've watched it before, it still chokes me up."

I decided to pose a question to her about writing a story about my life. "Do you think my story is worth telling?" I asked. She responded, "Louis, that would be amazing. I think there are a lot of people who would identify with the struggles you encountered to accomplish your personal, family and career goals. Your story would motivate teens, help parents, and inspire professionals who work with poor families and children. I thought about Latisha's comments for a few minutes and responded, "A story about my early childhood, teenage years and adult life might be interesting. I think there are many young parents, educators, and social service workers who would benefit from hearing my story. It may give teens motivation to pursue their dreams, provide insight to families and help professionals who work with children in poverty." That's where my story begins.

PART I

CHAPTER 1

INTRODUCTION

I had read numerous books during my lifetime and enjoyed various genres. My only exposure to writing was what I learned in high school English class and from observing teachers when I worked as a teacher aide in a small Alternative Education Program. I wasn't interested in writing a romance, science, or mystery novel. I wanted to write a book that was fictional but included real people, places, and events. To blend a story that wasn't true with facts that were historically and chronologically accurate posed a challenge for me.

As I began to write, I had to continually remind myself that I was writing a story about me from my youth to old age. The chapters about my education, work experiences, family and real life situations were meshed together in a seventy-year timeline. To span a period of time that long and include real events that had an impact on me was difficult. To overcome the challenge, I combined fictional chapters with non-fictional chapters, divided them into five parts and concluded each part with chapters about family/friends and discussions (interludes) with Latisha.

Before I started to write, I drove to the local Best Buy and bought a new laptop computer. The one I had been using for ten years was on its last legs. I wanted an up-to-date computer that would make writing easier.

My first step was to use the internet to find recommendations for beginning writers. Google and Wikipedia became my best friends.

I wanted to write a story that was interesting and educational. There were many articles and books to consult. I found one titled, *10 Secrets to Write Better Stories* written by Joe Bunting. [1]

Bunting identified and described each of the secrets as follows:

1. Write three drafts in three months.
2. Develop your protagonist.
3. Create suspense and drama.
4. Show don't tell.
5. Write a good dialogue.
6. Write about death.
7. Edit like a pro.
8. Know the rules, then break them.
9. Defeat writer's block.
10. Share your work.

As I wrote, I tried to adhere to these "secrets." I realized that writing a first draft in three months might be difficult, unless I cloistered myself in an attic, left only to eat, sleep, and take care of hygiene needs. During the first month, I wrote twenty-five pages. My goal was to meet the three-month recommendation.

The second recommended "secret" was to develop a protagonist. I felt comfortable with the book's main character. His determination to inspire others was presented initially in the prologue and gradually developed from his early years until his retirement. Louis continually searched for a better life despite unforeseen obstacles.

Creating suspense and drama was the third recommended secret to good writing. I understood the concept and tried to develop both in each chapter. As an avid reader, I recognized readers would not enjoy my book unless they wanted to find out the character's outcomes.

The "show don't tell" secret was a difficult technique to master. There was a tendency to "tell" too much and not describe the scene. I decided that citing examples and making comments would offer readers the opportunity to create visual images of situations that Louis encountered during his early years until retirement.

Writing good dialogue was dependent on the knowledge of my characters. Character development over a long period of time (seventy years) was a challenge because the character's situations changed so frequently. There were influences along the way...health, love, or sorrow that created the need to alter the dialogue to meet the changes.

The sixth "secret" was to write about death. This surprise element was used throughout the story. I recognized that readers would want to know what happens to characters during a story. Death was not difficult to write; the how and when were more important in holding a reader's interest.

Secret seven...writing three drafts was easier said than done. The obvious reason was to know when a draft was finished. I often did not know when to quit. I felt questions were left unanswered. Did I miss something? Should I change something? What did I forget? How can I make it better? The answers to these questions still existed when I finished my story.

Knowing the rules then breaking them was the eighth "secret." A writer tries to follow all the rules...grammar, punctuation, clarity, conciseness, and vocabulary. All rules should be respected, however, I found that sometimes a story may require a different set of rules that might not be accepted by my readers. I decided to follow my own example...let it happen!

Writer's block was something that most storytellers encounter. The recommendation was to just keep writing even though the writing didn't seem good. Don't try to be perfect, just write. As I wrote, I was fortunate that words flowed freely. Sentences and paragraphs flowed rapidly and sequentially.

The tenth and final "secret" was to share your work, despite the possibility of failure. I was forced to write the best story I could. I decided to include "Interludes" at the end of each chapter. I used the strategy to share my progress with Latisha. Her feedback helped me stay on track and obtain another point of view.

During my research, I found that there were many authors/writers who make recommendations to new writers. The ten secrets discussed are just examples of many possible options to consider when learning how to write. I felt that my attention to the "secrets" would prove beneficial to the success of my novel.

Idea

I read that writing a book required an *idea.* I felt comfortable about my book plan, and the direction I wanted to take. I questioned, what holds a reader's attention? Why do some books motivate readers to continue reading or stop entirely? For me, a book must capture my attention immediately. There must be a "hook." What would mine be?

I had given a lot of thought about who my readers would be. A book's genre often determines its readers. This book does not offer a reader a mystery to solve, an adventure to duplicate or a romance to fanaticize. It is a non-fictional novel that depicts the life story of a teen growing up in a big city and dealing with personal, local, and national issues related to poverty.

My purpose was to engage a reader in an imaginative and real experience. The question posed is…Who are my readers? My goal was to write a book that targets a small population like teens, parents, teachers, counselors, psychologists, and social workers.

To achieve my objectives, I developed a chronological timeline that captured Louis's life experiences from his early years to his retirement. Consideration was given to the development of timeline charts, an explanation of writing principles and a description of literary devices.

Timeline

To achieve continuity and order, I developed a chapter outline. The outline is divided into five parts that include Louis's age, year, school, and work details. The novel traced Louis's early childhood (five to fourteen), high school, (fourteen to eighteen), early work experiences (eighteen to twenty-four), higher education (twenty-one to thirty-five), marriage (thirty-seven to seventy), later work experiences (twenty-three to sixty-five), personal tragedies (thirty to seventy-one), family life (thirty-five to seventy-one) and retirement (sixty-five to seventy-one).

Each chapter corresponds with Louis's age, year, school, and work. For example, the chapter on *Cultural Influences* describes the national, state, and local events that occurred in the '60s. Each description is historically and chronologically accurate. I ended each event with a comment and its personal effect on me.

PART I

1 Prologue	71	2021	NA	Retired
CHAPTER	*AGE*	*YEAR*	*SCHOOL*	*WORK*
2 Introduction	71	2021	NA	Retired
3 Early Years	0 to 14	1950 to 1964	Elementary/ Junior High	NA
4 High School	14 to 18	1964 to 1968	DuSable High School	NA
5 Cultural Influences	18 to 24	1968 to 1974	City College	Teacher Aide
6 Transition	18	1968	"	"
7 Career Decisions	22	1972	"	"
8 Unexpected Event	22	1972	"	"
Interlude One	23	1973	"	"

PART II

CHAPTER	*AGE*	*YEAR*	*SCHOOL*	*WORK*
9 Graduation	24	1974	City College	Teacher Aide
10 Nature vs Nurture	24	1974	"	"
11 Career Path	24	1974	"	"
12 Goals Achieved	25	1975	"	"
13 Work and School	26	1976	"	"
14 Set Back	26	1976	"	"
15 Back on Track	26	1976	"	"
Interlude Two	26	1976	"	"

PART III

CHAPTER	*AGE*	*YEAR*	*SCHOOL*	*WORK*
16 Presidential Election	26 to 30	1976 to 1980	City College	Teacher Aide
17 Internship	28	1978	"	"
18 Part of the Job	29	1979	"	"
19 Job Offer	30	1980	University of Chicago	Chicago Child Care Society
20 Family Update	30	1980 to 1984	"	"
21 Reporting for Duty	34	1984	"	"
22 Jimmy	34	1984	"	"
23 Different Proposal	36	1986	"	"
24 Latisha	36 to 42	1986 to 1992	"	"
Interlude Three	38	1988	"	"

PART IV

CHAPTER	*AGE*	*YEAR*	*SCHOOL*	*WORK*
25 Research Proposal	34	1984	U of C	CCCS
26 New Job	36	1986	"	U of C
27 Foster Kids	38	1988	"	"

28 Master's Degree	44	1994	"	"
29 University of Chicago	44 to 65	1994 to 2016	"	"
30 September 11	65	2001	"	"
31 Family Update	71	2001	"	"
32 Neighborhood Return	71	2001	"	"
Interlude Four	71	2001	"	"

PART V

CHAPTER	*AGE*	*YEAR*	*SCHOOL*	*WORK*
33 The Clinic	46 to 63	1996 to 2013	Not Applicable	U of CSS
34 Food and Nutrition	43 to 66	1993 to 2016	"	"
35 KID's Count	65	2016	"	Retired
36 Presidents and Poverty	65 to 69	2016 to 2020	"	"
37 Retirement	65	2016	"	"
38 Donald J. Trump	71	2021	"	"
39 COVID – 19	71	2021	"	"
40 Joe Biden	71	2021	"	"
41 January 6, 2021	71	2021	"	"
42 Family/Friend Update	71	2021	"	"
Interlude Five	71	2021	"	"
43 Equity and Equality	71	2021	"	"
44 Conclusion	71	2021	"	"
Epilogue	71	2021	"	"
Charts/Figures/ Sources	71	2021	"	"
Post Preface	71	2021	"	"

Writing Principles

The basic principles of writing fiction or nonfiction include point of view, characterization, plot and conflict. Each of these principles can be used in many different ways to make a story distinctively different than anyone else's.

Point of view determines how the story will be told or narrated. A story may be told in first person, using the pronoun "I," second person using the pronoun "you," or third person using the pronouns "he," "she," or "they." First person narration offers the writer a sense of control but also provides limited flexibility because the narrative is restrained by the character's singular experience. Second person narration is used when a narrator within a story is speaking to another character. In a third person story the narrator tells someone else's story from the outside.

My story, of course, is told from the first person point of view. Louis narrates his own story from his own observations and opinions. His family, education and work experiences have a significant impact on his beliefs and career choices.

The second writing principle is *characterization.* It signifies human experiences that include body, mind and social circumstances. In my story, Louis is conscious of his father's heart condition and the likelihood that it may be genetic. He continually expresses his feelings about helping his family and families and children in poverty. The cultural, educational, work and political experiences that he encountered during his lifetime allows the reader to visualize the community and the neighborhood where he lived.

A third writing principle is *plot.* It equates to events that a character experiences. The negative and positive events in Louis's life begin early and continue through his adult life. He is faced with an early life tragedy that influences his character and how he reacts to future life experiences.

These experiences continue to build and rise in action and character development that reach a climax at the peak of the character's life and then make a decent resolution.

The fourth writing principle is *conflict.* It can be internal or external and is often referred to as what disturbs the main character. During Louis's life, he was faced with many life altering decisions that would influence the direction his life would take. His education and career decisions were often compelling and difficult. At times his decisions were not to his advantage, yet in many circumstances he chose wisely.

I realized that the four writing principles were interwoven and needed to work together to influence each other. If the story focuses on the main character then it will define the story's events. As Louis's character developed, the events fell into a line that developed the plot and the conflicts he encountered. [2]

Literary Devices

Literary devices are used in almost every novel. I was familiar with *simile* and metaphor but needed to learn how to use these and others in my story. I learned that literary devices are techniques used to create a special and pointed effect, to convey information and to help readers understand at a deeper level.

A *simile* is a figure of speech used to comparison of one thing with another (e.g., "as fierce as a tiger" or "crazy like a fox.") A *metaphor* is also a figure of speech in which a word or phrase is applied to an object or action but which is not literal. (e.g., "raining cats and dogs," "a heart of gold.") Other examples of literary devices include *foreshadowing, symbolism, and personification.* [3]

The research devoted to the *introductory* chapter was designed to help me write this story. As mentioned, I had learned about story parts in my high school English class and observed teachers in the Alternative Education Program but was still insecure about writing a novel.

As I wrote, I began to sense that the book had taken on a new objective. My original purpose was to tell an inspirational story about a character growing up in poverty during the 1960s. With the inclusion of a personal design, the book took on a dual purpose. One, being entertainment and the other education. Let's see what happens.

CHAPTER 2

EARLY YEARS

I took my first breath of life on March 28, 1950, at Chicago Med. I was the first of four siblings. My brother Peter, and sisters Rosie and Mindy were born within two years of each other. The closeness in age helped bind my family and provided a model that I used with my own family. The sign on the front door of our house read, "Welcome to The Van Patton Home."

My early childhood was uneventful. I felt secure with the love of my parents, sibling relationships and neighborhood friendships. I recall special occasions like birthdays, Christmas and summer vacations. The years and seasons flew by quickly...winter, snow and ice activities, spring outdoor bicycling, summer baseball and fall football.

Strict religious practice within our family did not exist. We attended the local Presbyterian church almost every Sunday. My parents weren't "bible belters" but believed that with faith in God their children would grow up possessing high values and morals. My parents raised us to view everyone individually and without prejudice or discrimination.

We lived in a beautiful neighborhood filled with children of all ages and ethnicities. I played daily with my white, black, and brown friends. We got along well with one another. There was an occasional disagreement that ended up in a wild wrestling match that lasted less than five minutes. Such incidents were forgotten quickly, as if they never occurred.

I attended Ray Elementary School from first through sixth grade. I credit my hard working teachers for providing a strong educational foundation that benefited me for my entire life. I think their dedication provided the motivation to complete high school and pursue higher education options.

Our family was considered middle class because we lived on the south side of Chicago in an area named Hyde Park. The area was defined as affluent. My father and mother's parents were of Dutch ancestry and immigrated to Chicago in the 1800s, like many of the families in the neighborhood. My parents worked hard to achieve the proverbial American dream. They had steady incomes because they had good paying blue-collar jobs.

My father was a foreman in a steel plant and my mother worked at a meat packing house. Because they inherited a strong work ethic, we were afforded advantages that most children did not have.

We vacationed every summer, attended concerts in the parks and enjoyed a variety of social and cultural events. My parents frequented the South Side nightclubs, dance parlors and music halls regularly with neighborhood friends.

After elementary school, I attended Canter Junior High with the same friends I had known for years. My education was important to me, and I began to sense that helping others would be my chosen career. I hoped that my high school years would follow suit.

Junior High ('62)

The 1960s began with a change in schools. I completed my elementary years successfully and was excited about attending junior high. Carter Junior High was in our neighborhood. Just ten blocks from my house. There were no yellow buses back then, and the school was populated with mostly white kids. There were a minority of black and brown kids whose parents worked in the nearby factories. Each day began with a stop at a friend's house. I remember the customary scream we made at each house, as we made our way to school… "O Johnny or O Jimmy!"

I walked to my new school every day with my friends, stopping along the way for penny candy at a local delicatessen, a game of street stickball and stone throwing at chestnut trees to knock down the "kinger" of chestnuts. It was a popular fall pastime that we loved. The challenge was to find the best chestnut, bore a hole in the middle of it with a hammer and nail, tie a shoestring through the hole and take turns trying to crush the chestnut. The chestnut that survived was the "kinger" of all chestnuts and the owner's winner was regarded with high esteem.

Baseball was another favorite summer pastime for "our gang." We all thought we would be major leaguers one day. In 1959, the White Sox won the American league pennant by defeating the Cleveland Indians at South Side's Comiskey Park. The "Sox" earned a bid to the world series. They played the Los Angeles Dodgers, but, unfortunately, they lost the series in six games.

We followed the team's progress; player's batting averages and number of hits every day. Our favorite players were the "Big Klu", 6 ft. 2 in. first baseman Ted Kluszewski, shortstop Luis Aparicio and second baseman Nellie Fox. Although we lost the series, the Sox were Chicago's team and the pride and joy of the South Side. [4]

One summer, our sandlot team decided to play ball in the Police Athletic League (PAL). We needed an adult sponsor to sign our team up. We were able to get one of the older teens to be our sponsor. He approached a local house builder and asked for shirts, hats, bats, and balls. We were all shocked when the builder said, "Yes." We practiced daily readying ourselves for the opportunity to play in a local park instead of a sandlot. Our first game was scheduled but did not occur. Wally, our sponsor, was late in signing us up, so we did not get the chance of a lifetime to play outside our neighborhood. We became known as one of the only neighborhood teams that wore uniforms when playing sandlot baseball. Of course, none of us made the majors, but we did learn how to calculate batting averages. Our math teacher was impressed when she taught the percentage unit. There were many other pastimes that we engaged in that will always be fond memories.

JFK ('60)

In November 1960, John Fitzgerald Kennedy was elected President. I was ten years old and in the seventh grade. Our country was excited about his election because he was an energetic young man, and married to a beautiful woman. Many described the couple as America's royalty. They made the worldwide newspapers every day.

I recall, prior to the Kennedy family, that I paid little attention to local, national, or worldwide politics or events. My daily existence centered around playing with my friends, engaging in all sports, going to school and eating junk food.

Cuban Missile Crisis ('62)

The headline read, "Cuba Showdown Near; Russia Warns of War." It was October 22, 1962. My friends and I started our day the same as any other. But today seemed different. When we arrived at school, you could sense fear and tension on our teachers' faces. It was the beginning of a new school year, and I had just turned twelve years old. I anticipated that eighth grade would fly by, and I would finally get to high school. A goal I had dreamt about for several years. When I finally realized the severity of what was happening, I began to question if I would get to high school. [5]

Most of my friends seemed unconcerned about the headline or the crisis itself. I became overly concerned and felt that event was extremely serious. I began reading more about what was named the "Bay of Pigs' crisis. The incident occurred in Cuba. I knew the country was close to Florida but did not realize it was only ninety miles away. I learned that the president of Cuba was Fidel Castro, and he was placing missiles from the Soviet Union president Nika Khrushchev on Cuban bases with the threat of a nuclear war. The United States trusted neither Cuba nor the Soviet Union and wanted the missiles removed. President Kennedy planned an invasion at the Bay of Pigs. The invasion was botched, and the nuclear threat continued.

The threat of war with Russia became so likely, that panic and fear influenced many people to build bomb shelters in a number of states and cities. Chicago followed suit. The atomic age was born and brought Chicago into a period of anxiety. It was an era of bomb shelters. There were city-wide discussions about where to build shelters. A limestone quarry in the Bridgeport neighborhood and an underground garage in Grant Park were being considered as options. I read an accounting of a boy my age who was excited about a new swimming pool being built in his neighborhood. It turned out to be a bomb shelter.

My parent's reaction to the crisis and shelter craze was discussed openly at the supper table. They were extremely concerned about the outcome of the crisis and its effect on my siblings and me. I realized later that they played the crisis down, so that we would go about our daily routines as if it were not serious, and that the crisis would end without the end of civilization.

The world waited for thirteen days before the nuclear crisis ended. President Kennedy negotiated an agreement to avert a catastrophe. The Soviet Union agreed to dismantle the Cuban weapon sites in an exchange that the US would not invade Cuba. The world, the US and Chicago were at ease, but the possible threat of war with the Soviet Union continued in the guise of the "Cold War.

JFK's concern for poverty was expressed throughout his presidency. He became overtly concerned and his efforts included the expansion of the federal surplus commodities program in an effort to feed the nation's hungry. He signed the Area Redevelopment Act in 1961 that sent funds to three impoverished states...Pennsylvania, West Virginia, and Kentucky. In June 1961, Kennedy signed the Housing Act which expanded low- and middle-income housing for the elderly and urban renewal. In 1962, he signed the Public Welfare Amendments. It was designed to improve administration and reduce the number of people dependent on the Aid to Families with Dependent Children (AFDC). JFK was also credited for initiating the development of the domestic Peace Corp to fight poverty. [6]

Despite Kennedy's valiant efforts to combat poverty, he "never abandoned the idea of an offense against poverty." His measures inspired his brother, Robert and his successor, Lyndon Baynes Johnson (LBJ). [7]

Assassination ('63)

On November 22. 1963, while I was attending junior high, I witnessed a tragic national catastrophe…the assassination of President John F. Kennedy. His death had an impact on the entire country. His death affected me in many ways. Living a secure and loving family life had limited my exposure to tragedy and real-life experiences. The assassination traumatized me.

As a thirteen year old, politics were far removed from my mind. However, the death of "JFK" resonated with me. The Kennedy family reminded me of ours. Both John and Jackie Kennedy were in their mid-forties and had two young children. They seemed to engage in the same things that less famous families did. I often saw pictures on TV or in the newspaper that showed them enjoying outdoor activities like swimming, football and celebrating holidays. I felt a commonality with them…the concept of a loving family unit.

John Kennedy's assassination was the first tragedy that I experienced during my lifetime. I also realized that it would not be the last. The entire era was filled with experiences that strengthened my resilience to become a secure and contributing adult.

JFK's sudden and traumatic death and his efforts to pass legislation to help people in poverty struck a chord in me. Although I had little contact with poor families and children, I began to sense that my lack of interest would change.

On Friday, November 22, 1963, Lyndon B. Johnson (LBJ) took the oath of office on Air Force One with a composed yet tearful Jackie Kennedy by his side. He became the 36th US president.

LBJ hit the ground running. Since he served as Kennedy's vice president, he was well aware of JFK's efforts to help the poor. He coined his domestic plan "The Great Society" for all Americans. He championed programs like Medicare, Medicaid, Head Start, the Voting Rights Act, and the Civil Rights Act. The programs had a profound impact on health, education and civil rights. Despite his impressive achievements, Johnson's legacy was marred by his failure to lead America out of the Vietnam War.

Johnson actively pursued a "War on Poverty." He pushed Congress to pass legislation attacking literacy, unemployment, and racial discrimination. He obtained his firsthand feelings about poverty and discrimination while teaching disadvantaged Mexican American students. His exposure to families and children in poverty made a deep impression on him and a lifelong desire to help the poor.

My limited exposure to politics while in junior high changed when I started high school. JFK's assassination and the leadership of LBJ inspired me to take an in-depth interest in American poverty. The first two years at Hyde Park High gave me an opportunity to learn about Kennedy's dreams and Johnson's realities.

Eighth Grade ('63-'64)

I had one year left at Canter Junior High before going to high school. I looked forward to attending Hyde Park Academy High School. My friends and I were excited about participating in city-wide sports, parties, meeting new friends and gaining the independence associated with being a "high schooler."

On September 6,1963, as was customary in the Chicago city school district, we returned to school the day after Labor Day. I had just turned thirteen and welcomed the "teenage" label. I looked around my homeroom and saw the same faces that I had known for eight years. My eyes wandered around the room; I noticed an unfamiliar face. She was sitting next to the window in the first row close to my friend, Jeff. She was about my height. She had long black hair, blue eyes, and a dark complexion. The homeroom bell rang, and we marched to our first period class…math. Out of the corner of my eye, I noticed that "she" was following me. Are we in the same first period class? Yes, we were. The class ended and I walked to English class. Disappointedly, I didn't see her again for the rest of the day.

When I got home from school, I noticed a moving van in front of a newly sold house. There she was sitting on the front porch watching the movers and twirling a strand of her straight and shiny dark hair. I hadn't paid much attention to girls that I knew in the neighborhood. They didn't play sports or hang around with my friends or me. I guess they did their thing whatever that was.

I wasn't shy when it came to expressing myself with friends, family, or relatives. Did I have the courage to cross the street and to say "hi?" I didn't. The next day I saw her at school and learned her name was Susan. One day she stood next to her locker when I walked by. This time, I decided I would muster the courage to introduce myself. As I got closer to the locker and noticed she was even prettier than I had first noticed. I walked tentatively toward her. My heart began to beat like a drum and beads of sweat were forming on my forehead. What was happening? Nervously, I said, "Hi, my name is Louis." I was shaking like a leaf. I am sure she noticed. She said, "hi" to me and asked, "Are you going to math class?" I said, "yes." The encounter was my first experience talking to a girl. During the year, we became close friends and enjoyed talking, helping each other with homework, and eating ice cream at the local soda shop. I sensed that girls were more than OK and looked forward to the social life that high school would offer.

School Boycott ('63)

In 1963, there was a mass boycott and demonstration against the segregation and unequal conditions in white and black school policies in the Chicago Public Schools. More than 225,000 students boycotted and called for the resignation of school superintendent Benjamin Willis. Half of the entire school district stayed home, and more than ten thousand people crowded City Hall and the Board of Education buildings, demanding integration of the city's schools. **8**

I read about the demonstration and watched the protests on TV. Because the boycott had no effect on me, I paid little attention to it. I did learn that many city schools populated with a majority of white students had better teaching and learning conditions than those schools populated by black students. Because I lived in a mostly white neighborhood and attended a partially integrated high school, the overcrowded classrooms, lack of books and the physical conditions of the all-black schools had little impact on me. I hoped that when I attended high school my situation would remain the same.

In June, I graduated from eighth grade and wished that I had a summer job. I talked to my father about it, and he suggested I mow lawns. We had a push mower that I used on our lawn. It cut well but sure required a lot of work. Regardless, I gave it a try. I advertised my availability on a flyer and walked up and down the street placing it in our neighbor's mailboxes. The first day, I got two phone calls and two jobs. I had a total of six jobs for the summer. I charged a dollar for each lawn. By the middle of the summer, I had made twenty-four dollars. Certainly not a lot of money but having my own business felt good. The hard work made me realize that there was a payoff, and if I wanted to be successful, I would need to put my "nose to the grindstone."

One day, I came home from mowing early and heard my parents talking at the kitchen table about their jobs. My mother mentioned that the meat packing plant might be closing, and she would be out of a job. My father was equally concerned because his steel plant job was also in jeopardy. A few weeks later, I read that both plants would survive and the possibility of my parents losing their jobs was put on hold for a year.

The summer flew by. I continued my lawn business and made more than fifty dollars. I declared that I was a rich man! I spent most of it on new clothes. I wanted to be in style at my new school. I bought a pair of dungarees, khakis, two solid color T-shirts, and two button- down collar shirts... one plaid and one with stripes. I felt armed and ready for whatever high school had to offer.

During the '60s, the Beatles, a band from England, was at the top of the music charts singing songs named "I Want to Hold Your Hand" and "Hard Day's Night." I wasn't a big fan of their music. I had become more interested in listening to soul music. Groups like the Supremes and Platters from "Motown" Detroit. My favorite teenage TV program was American Bandstand. It was on every day and hosted by Dick Clark. I was a daily viewer and enjoyed watching the shows' "elite." The regulars became teenage celebrities. I watched brown-eyed, brown-hair Arlene, pert, blond, Justine, suave Bob and handsome Kenny dance to the music each day after school. [9]

Another teenage pastime was the movies. My friends and I would walk to the neighborhood theater on Saturday nights. We all liked action movies and chose "Bullitt" with Steve McQueen, "McLintock" John Wayne and "Fist Full of Dollars" with Clint Eastwood. Before entering the seating area we loaded up with popcorn, cokes, jujubes, and milk duds. We had to be well supplied for two hours. Of course, we noticed a group of girls seated close to us in another section. Close enough so that we could "spy" on one another. [10]

Just before high school started, I heard about the possibility of getting a paper route in the neighborhood. I asked my friend Johnny about it. "Yes, Joey got a job at the movie theater and was giving up his route," he said. I found out where he lived and within a week, I had the evening route. I could hardly believe it! I ran home to tell my parents the good news. They were excited for me and wished the best. I worked the route for my first two years of high school. Weather was a factor in getting the job done. I sweated during the summer and froze in the winter. The spring and fall months were enjoyable.

CHAPTER 3

HIGH SCHOOL

Freshman ('64'65)

I entered the huge, bronze-colored doors with gusto. I met up with my friends from the neighborhood and waited in the hallway for the bell to ring. We didn't wait long before a familiar blaring and booming noise pierced our ears. High school had begun! We walked to our homerooms, received our class schedules, listened to announcements, and waited for the first period bell. I entered the crowded hallway and immediately realized that the number of students was greater and more diverse than junior high.

The long anticipated high school experience had arrived! I attended each class religiously. To skip a class was a mortal sin. My parents worked hard so that my brother, sisters, and I would have an opportunity to go to college. Also, since I was an athlete, missing a class or skipping school were grounds for after-school suspension and removal from a sport. My favorite subject was math. I was good with numbers and had little trouble grasping the concepts. Now, English was a different story.

During my first year, I participated in three sports: football in the fall, basketball in the winter and baseball in the spring. I guess you could say I was a "jock." There were other classifications like nerds (intelligent kids), squeaks (wore current clothing styles), rocks (soft gangs) and motor heads (auto mechanics). My label fit perfectly.

Our school held weekly Saturday night teen activities in the gym. The gym was divided into two sections. One side for dancing and the other side for boys' basketball. I imagine that girls could have crossed over, but none ever did. The school sponsored dances throughout the year like Harvest Moon in the fall, Snowball in the winter and Mayday in the spring. I didn't attend any of the dances. Looking back, I sure wish I had. My freshman year passed quickly. I liked my classes and teachers, enjoyed participating in sports and hanging out with my friends.

My first year of high school ended in mid-June, and I began looking for a summer job. A neighborhood grocery had a help wanted sign on its window, so I walked in and asked to apply for the job. I was told that it was part time (twenty hours a week) and paid $2.50 an hour. I was given the title "bagger" and spent most of my four days placing food in customer's bags. One day I was told to work in the basement unpacking cereal from large boxes. Each box had twelve boxes filled with "Wheaties." I didn't get any instructions and was given a box cutter. I cut into the top of my first box and realized that I slashed the tops of four cereal boxes. I hid the box and made sure that my future cuts were done right.

I worked for the grocer the rest of the summer and saved a lot of my earnings. I knew that I wanted to buy some new clothes and thought my sophomore expenses would increase. I planned on expanding my interest in the opposite sex. I might even ask a girl to go to a school dance.

Sophomore ('65-'66)

My sophomore year began similarly to my freshman year. I attended classes, played sports and hung out...with one exception...the new girl in the front row. Our teacher asked Julie to hand out books to everyone. As she walked down each row, I watched her every movement. She was cute, petite, and polite. She handed me my book, and I thanked her. She said, "You're welcome." My mind raced, "How could I introduce myself?" Our teacher gave us an assignment at the end of class, and I wrote everything down on a piece of paper. Was that page 6 through 10 or 6 through 12? Julie walked toward my desk, and I asked her what the assignment was. She said tersely, "6 through 12."

We walked out of the classroom together, and I headed to math. We were walking in the same direction, and I realized that we were in the same class. That was the beginning of my realization that girls were more than OK. Julie and I continued to get to know each other throughout the year. We went to movies, dances and helped each other with homework. It turned out to be a great year, especially, since I had my first girlfriend.

Shock ('66)

As I approached our house, I noticed an ambulance in the driveway. I panicked and ran as fast as I could. I walked up the driveway; two women were hovering over my father. He was lying on the front lawn face up. In the background, I saw my mother crying and held by two neighbors. I was in shock! My body began to tremble. I ran to my mother and tried to comfort her. One of the two women attending to my father walked toward us. Her facial expression indicated her news was not going to be positive. She said, "We tried to revive him but could not. It was a massive heart attack." My father was dead!

Tears trickled down my cheeks, as I tried to console my mother. She wailed in agony and cried uncontrollably. With the help of neighbors, we got her into the house and sat her on a living room chair. My brother and two sisters weren't home from school yet. I knew my mother would not want them to see their father lying on the front lawn. He was pronounced deceased on the scene and was placed on a bed in my parents' bedroom.

My father's sudden death was traumatic. I realized how hard he had worked, his commitment to me and my siblings and the love of his house and neighborhood. Later, my mother told me that she had walked my father to the front door and kissed him on the cheek. She watched him walk to the car.

He was on his way to the steel plant to work his 3:00 to 11:00 afternoon shift. Within moments, he shriveled to the ground and laid there motionless. She ran to him. It was too late. He was just forty-five and there were no indicators that he had heart disease, although his father died from a heart attack also. I thought, a heart is like a clock, it stops ticking when the battery runs out.

"What do we now?" I asked my mother. My father's income was essential to living in our neighborhood. Without it, that possibility was impossible. "Will we have to move?" I asked my mother. Her answer was, "yes." I felt my life come to a screeching halt. It meant that I would go to a new school and leave the secure neighborhood that I grew up in.

The summer weeks and months before we moved were terrifying. I realized that I would need to make new friends and get used to a new high school. I questioned, "Would I fit in? Will I make new friends? Would l like my new school and home"? I continued to work at the grocery store that summer to help my mother with the bills. The additional income offered little help to pay off the mounting bills.

My mother sold our house quickly. Many white families were leaving the city and moving to the suburbs. Realtors were eager to market our house for less than its true value. I found out that many of the white families were moving because thousands of black families were migrating from the south and relocating in cities like Chicago. The term coined for the movement was known as "white flight." [11]

My mother struggled to find housing, and because of her limited income, we could not continue to live in the Hyde Park area. We ended up finding a two-bedroom apartment in the Robert Taylor Housing Project for low-income households on the south side of Chicago. Our new home had two bedrooms. My brother Peter and I shared a room, and my mother shared her room with my two sisters Rosie and Mindy.

The projects were sixteen-story high-rise buildings, and our apartment was on the thirteenth-floor, number 1300. Over ninety percent of the residents were black. The projects possessed an extremely high concentration of poverty, gang violence, drug addiction and high crime rates. Most residents were unemployed and needed public financial assistance. The buildings were poorly maintained, neglected, and underserved by the city and housing department.

The effects of our new housing were traumatic for me. I had always lived in a single-family home in a safe racially-mixed neighborhood. Adjusting to the projects was difficult. The building was overcrowded, the apartments were small, poorly heated, and rat infested. My mother did her best to keep the apartment clean and rodent free. I had lived and played with many ethnic and racially diverse kids over the years, but to live in an environment that was predominantly black was new to me. I felt no racial bias and tried to adjust as much as possible.

Living and going to high school in the Fuller Park area of Chicago was an eye opening experience. Poverty existed in the projects, on the streets and in the schools. My mother and I struggled to make ends meet and longed to find a way to return to Hyde Park. We had no idea what the future held.

Junior Year ('66-'67)

The first night in our new "home" was frightening. The noise throughout the building was deafening...women screaming, children crying and men yelling. Outside, sirens blared, cars screeched to a halt and shots rang out. I had a difficult time getting to sleep. When I finally did, I dreamt of our Hyde Park home and neighborhood.

My new school was named DuSable High School. It was named after Jean Baptiste Point DuSable, a Haitian-born fur trader, recognized as the founder of Chicago. There were more than 4,000 students enrolled and two graduation ceremonies were required in the spring and summer. Eighty percent of the student population were residents of the Robert Taylor Housing Project. The school was known for its gang activity and violence.

My brother Peter and I walked to our new school not knowing what to expect. Peter was fourteen and in his first year of high school. He had enjoyed the comforts of growing up with terrific parents in a great neighborhood. Peter was slight of build, shy, and had a difficult time expressing himself. He was diagnosed with a heart murmur when he was five. Going to a new school was more traumatic for him than me. As his big brother, I felt the need to protect him.

We reached our new school after a twenty-minute walk. I looked at the school in awe. Its size was overwhelming. It resembled a huge department store with hundreds of windows. We entered the bronze-colored, steel, double front doors with hundreds of other students. All eager to meet up with their friends and begin a new school year. Peter walked ahead of me as I observed the overcrowded hallways that were nearly impassable. My initiation to my new school was to witness a fight between a white and black kid. The fight was quickly broken up. I watched two school resource officers escort the bloodied kids to the principal's office. My introduction to the housing projects and high school had begun with noteworthy incidents. I feared what I would encounter next.

I escorted Peter to his homeroom on the first floor. My homeroom was on the third floor, Room 321. The announcements were barely heard over the PA system because of all the noise. I looked at my schedule and found my first period class and room…history, Room 342. I walked toward the room shoulder to shoulder with my new classmates hoping that that I would find the room quickly. Moving as slowly as a turtle, the room number suddenly appeared above a door frame. I entered the room, found a seat and waited for the teacher to begin class. The class went surprisingly well. The remainder of the day was uneventful. I told Peter that we would meet near the DuSable statue at the end of the day. As I walked toward the statue, I saw Peter waiting patiently. "How was your first day," I asked? He said, "Fine."

We walked toward the projects, neither of us saying much. The pressure and stress of the day left the both of us tongue-tied.

All went well the first couple weeks. I adjusted to the new school and made a couple of friends. Unlike Hyde Park, I decided not to participate in sports. The decision was a tough one, but one I needed to make, so I could find a job to help my mother. Finding a job in the neighborhood wasn't easy. I searched for days, knocking on the doors of grocers, hardware shops and clothing stores. I found nothing. I realized that helping my mother was essential. I had to find a money maker.

Peter and I took the same route home from school to our home about the same time every day. One day, I noticed a group of black kids congregating near a corner drug store. There were five boys and one girl. She looked familiar. I realized we were in the same intermediate algebra class. Her name was Angie. The next day, she approached me, and asked if I would help her with her homework. I said, "Sure, how about in the study hall today?" She accepted. We met for thirty minutes. She struggled with every problem. I thought math wasn't her strength. We met a couple more times to no avail. She just didn't get it.

I met Angie outside of school a few days later. She approached me and thanked me for my help. She said that she had decided to change her math class. She commented that I was a good teacher, and she was a bad student. Recognizing that I was good with numbers, she asked if I wanted a job. "What kind of job?" I asked. She said, ``My brother needs help with his business. "What business is he in? "I asked. It's better that you don't know," she said. "What do I need to do?" I asked. She said, "I will let you know tomorrow."

The next day, Angie gave me an envelope filled with papers. "My brother wants you to follow the directions inside." she said. "When does he want them back?" I asked. "Can you finish the work in two days?" she asked. I looked at the directions and counted the number of sheets. "Yeah, I can," I said. When I got home, I started working on more than fifty papers filled with columns of numbers that had to be added. subtracted and multiplied in an accounting fashion. The work was new to me, but I finished in five hours. I gave the envelope back to Angie the next day. She was surprised that I finished so fast. "What do you think? Would you like the job?" she asked. I said, "I do need money." "How much does the job pay?" I asked. "My brother told me to offer you fifty dollars a week," she responded. "You got a deal," I said. I walked away with a huge smile, not realizing what I was getting into.

The next day, Angie approached me outside of school. "There are a few things that you need to do," she said "What?" I asked. "Don't tell anyone, don't make copies and don't ask questions!" she spoke. I sensed that something was illegal, but I needed money to help my mother, so I agreed. After a couple of months, Angie said that her brother was pleased with my work. "By the way, he nicknamed you numbers," she spoke. I chuckled. "I do have a couple of requests," I said. "I have been approached to join a gang. I think they need help too." I spoke. "What do you want?" she asked. "I want protection for my brother, Peter and me." "No, problem," she responded. I thought, what would my father think?

I had no knowledge of gangs and really didn't realize what I was getting into. I decided to find out what gangs were all about. I talked to a few people and began reading newspapers.

I read that the gang history in Chicago was old, dating back to the Civil War. The first gangs developed along ethnic lines...Poles, Italians and Irish. They were primarily competitive young men who wanted recognition for their firehouse. Early gangs were considered social clubs known for their toughness and rebellion. As the years passed, gangs were considered social clubs competing against one another for supremacy. They often engaged in "rumbles" (fights) and drag racing. [12]

A couple notable black gangs in the early sixties were the Blackstone Rangers, Vice Lords and Gaylords. There were also white and Puerto Rician gangs that competed with the black gangs for recruits and territory. In the mid-sixties the definition of gangs changed. Many became involved in drugs and violence, creating fear in many south side Chicago neighborhoods. I didn't know the name of the gang I was working for and truly didn't want to know. [13]

The weeks and months passed by quickly. I knew what I did was wrong and unlawful, but to help my mother and for my brother and me to survive, I had no other option. I continued a life of crime for the remainder of the school year, during the summer and during my senior year.

I began feeling somewhat comfortable at school. I went to some sporting events, a few parties and hung out with my new friends. The football team didn't play well. I think I could have been of some help. The basketball and baseball teams played well. Their games were exciting and both teams were leading their conferences.

There were house parties practically every weekend. I went to a few of them. Most of the kids enjoyed dancing and eating. A few drank alcohol and smoked pot. I wasn't into either. I met Josie at one of the parties. She was a junior in my English class. She was my height, blond and blue-eyed. We dated throughout the year. We hung out at the games, parties, and the movies.

During the two years that we dated, I never asked her to my home to meet my mother and sisters. My mother knew I had a girlfriend but did not pry. I was embarrassed with our living conditions and fearful something would happen to her. She never questioned my motive, I thought, she understood why.

Josie was conscientious and thoughtful. I soon realized she was someone special. We were both inexperienced with intimate relationships and this was a first for us. We realized we were young and that future "loves" would be part of growing up. We continued to date for the remainder of the year and during our senior year. The last time I saw Josie was at graduation. I often wonder what had become of her. I know one thing for sure, she was my first love and a memory that I cherished.

Although the neighborhood I was forced to live in was questionable, the south side of Chicago boasted an array of cultural and social offerings such as professional sports teams, music, landmark buildings, museums, educational/medical institutions, beaches and parks. Its residents enjoyed a variety of educational and entertaining pastimes, including performing arts, stand-up comedy, house music, blues, hip hop, gospel, jazz, and soul music.

Chicago became known for its hot dogs, pizza, and beef sandwiches. The naturally cased beef hot dogs were steamed or boiled, placed in a poppy seed bun, and smothered with yellow mustard, onions, tomatoes, relish and served with a large dill pickle. Another local favorite was deep-dish pizza. It had a raised outer crust and chunky tomato sauce on top of mozzarella cheese instead of underneath with your choice of toppings. Italian beef sandwiches were also a craving. The beef was thinly sliced, simmered in broth (gravy), topped with Italian seasoning, and served on a hard crusted roll. All three were favorites of mine before moving. I promised myself that I would eventually eat all three again.

When my family lived in Hyde Park, my parents would take advantage of the nightlife, and took my brother, sisters and me to the parks, beaches, museums, and Chicago White Sox baseball games. We enjoyed eating the local cuisine (dogs, pizza, beef). Those luxuries were in the past...I longed for the good old days. I was proud of living in Chicago and more so the South Side.

Senior Year (67'- '68)

My senior year was uneventful. I continued to date Josie. We enjoyed each other's company and realized that after graduation we would part company. We continued to attend sporting and school events, go to the movies and grab a burger and soda at McDonalds. I was thankful that she was part of my life during these difficult times. Attending classes and doing well were important to me. I was planning on graduating at the top of the class. I had no idea what my future held...work, college, or the armed services, but my conscience told me that hard work would pay off. I am not sure if my "inner drive" was learned or inherited. Regardless, I was determined to be successful and contribute to the neighborhood.

Graduation arrived quickly. I had fulfilled all the requirements and was eligible for the spring commencement. My mother and siblings were proud of my accomplishments and were excited about the ceremony. Because our class had two thousand graduates, the ceremony was held in the Chicago City Center. I had achieved my goal of graduating in the top ten percent of the class. I was proud of my accomplishment but had no idea of what the future held. Josie graduated also. It was the last time I saw her. My mother had a small party in our apartment. We enjoyed a homemade chocolate cake, vanilla ice cream and soda. As a gift, my mother gave me my father's wristwatch. It meant the world to me. I know he would be proud.

CHAPTER 4

CULTURAL INFLUENCES

The period between 1960 and the 1970s was historical, tumultuous, and controversial. The notable sixties began with the" Hippie" counterculture movement, included the Vietnam War '64, The Civil Rights Act '64 and the Freedom Movement in '65. I wasn't actively involved in any of the cultural events or movements. I heard or read about them in the newspaper. I am certain, however, that they had a direct impact on my future life. Here is how I remember them. [14]

Hippie Movement (60s and 70s)

The Hippie movement was defined as a counterculture rejection of mainstream American mores. It originated on college campuses throughout the United States. The hippies conducted sit-ins in public places to disrupt normal life in a nonviolent way. This subculture vehemently opposed the Vietnam War, supported women's liberation, and advocated civil rights for all. Hippies dressed unconventionally, favored communal living, ate organic foods, wore blue jeans, sandals and beads, believed in legalized marijuana, gay marriage, and single parenthood. The hippie cultural revolution had a significant impact on the Civil Rights Movement and opposition to the Vietnam War. [15]

The Hippie movement began when I was in junior high and continued past high school. As a twelve-year-old, with little exposure to the "outside" world, it had little effect on me. I read about it, but its visibility was nonexistent in our neighborhood and school. During my senior year of high school, some of the kids had adopted the hippie clothing styles, wore sandals and beads and voiced concerns about the Vietnam War.

I had become quite conscious of the war and followed the US involvement as a senior and after graduation. Each day TV news anchors would report the number of casualties and deaths. It was a frightening experience that haunts me to this day.

I held the belief that all wars were futile and that our country should not engage in other countries' civil wars. As an eighteen-year-old, I had to register with the Selective Service System. It was an independent agency of the US government that registers men for the draft. The draft was a lottery system to call men to service in a sequence determined by random lottery number and year of birth. Men were also examined for mental, physical, and moral fitness for military services. Men were given a random number between 1 and 366 corresponding with their birthdays. Lower numbers were called first. I was included in the 1971 lottery. Fortunately, my number was 349. I wasn't drafted nor did I enlist in a service. I knew a few of the guys in my neighborhood who were injured or killed in the war. I often questioned if I had been drafted would I have gone into the service? I heard that some draftees went to Canada, and others claimed to be pacifists. I am thankful I did not have to make that decision.

Civil Rights Act ('64)

Through the efforts of President Lyndon Baines Johnson (LBJ) in 1964, Congress passed the landmark civil rights and labor law and it was signed into law. It outlawed employment discrimination based on race, color, religion, sex, and national origin. It ended segregation in public schools including elementary, secondary, and public colleges and universities. The act also outlawed segregation in businesses, theaters, restaurants, and hotels. It was considered one of the crowning legislative achievements of the Civil Rights Movement. [16]

DuSable High School and the Robert Taylor Housing Projects were in the Fuller Park area on the south side. Both were predominantly black. I understood the discrimination issue and why both the school and housing were ninety percent black. If you lived in a black neighborhood, you attended a black school.

The year the Civil Rights Act became a law, I saw no change. Blacks continued to live in the segregated projects and attended all black schools. As years passed, changes did occur in the projects and schools. Because I lived and went to school under such conditions, I understood that if housing and school integration did not occur, the low standard of living for poor whites and blacks would continue to exist. Schools and housing would not improve.

Freedom Movement ('65)

"I Have a Dream" was a public speech delivered by Martin Luther King on August 28, 1963 on the steps of the Lincoln Memorial in Washington, DC. It was his signature theme that was synonymous with all his civil rights activities.

The Freedom Movement, also known as the Chicago Open House Movement, was led by civil rights leader Martin Luther King, Jr. (MLK). It was created to challenge systemic racial segregation and discrimination in Chicago and its suburbs. It included rallies, protests, marches, boycotts and other forms of nonviolent actions. Its goal was to integrate housing, correct educational deficiencies, influence income disparity, decrease unemployment, and improve health conditions caused by racism in the black community. The movement was credited with inspiring the Fair Housing Act passed by Congress in 1968, which addressed the issue of blacks being kept out of all white middle class neighborhoods. [17]

Assassination ('68)

A month before I graduated from high school, April 4, 1968, Martin Luther King was assassinated in Memphis TN. He was 39 years old. He was fatally shot while standing on a hotel second floor balcony. He was in Memphis to support an African American sanitation workers' strike. The news of his death initiated riots in cities across the United States. [18]

Chicago was no exception. The protesters were mostly black and many areas of the city were heavily damaged. King's death led to anger and disillusionment among them. Across the country, dozens of people were killed, and thousands were injured.

Living in a black neighborhood and going to a mostly all-black school provided a unique insight to MLK's death. I witnessed firsthand the effect that his assassination had on my black neighbors and friends. They had come to admire his civil rights efforts and looked to him as their saviour. I had been following him since the Civil Rights and Freedom Movements. I recognized the need for equality among poor whites and blacks. His death opened my eyes to the inequalities and inequities that existed in the US and my hometown.

Living and going to school in an area with segregated neighborhood boundaries provided an insight that most white teenagers could never comprehend. I learned about the plight of poor people, especially blacks. I recognized that my housing and school situations would impact my entire life.

Fair Housing Act ('68)

The Act was part of the Civil Rights Act of 1968. It expanded on previous acts and prohibited discrimination concerning the sale, rental, and financing of housing based on race, religion, national origin, sex, handicapped and family status. It became a reality after Martin Luther King's death. President Johnson used the national tragedy to urge congressional approval as a memorial to King's life work. It was aimed at addressing entrenched housing segregation. The Act was enforced by the Department of Housing and Urban Development (HUD). Its enactment was an improvement in combatting discrimination, although significant degrees of segregation still existed across much of the country. [19]

Because I lived in the projects, I had firsthand knowledge and concern for the blatant discrimination, bias and prejudice landlords and owners had against blacks and poor whites. I recall my mother not having rent for one month. An eviction notice was taped to our door. We were notified that payment was needed in fifteen days. I used my savings to prevent our having to live homeless. There were numerous other examples of the need for the Housing Act that I witnessed during my two years living in the projects. Most did not affect me directly but made an indelible impression that I carried with me for the rest of my life.

Chicago Eight ('68)

The Chicago Eight were charged by the United States federal government with conspiracy, crossing state lines with the intent to incite a riot and other charges related to anti-Vietnam War and countercultural protests in Chicago during the 1968 Democratic National Convention. Most were acquitted—seven of the eight for conspiracy, some were found guilty of traveling between states to incite a riot. [20]

I didn't pay much attention to the Chicago Eight incident. It certainly was not an issue that would have directly affected me. It did, however, add to the cultural influences of the era.

RFK ('68)

On June 6, 1968, Robert Francis Kennedy (RFK) was assassinated in Los Angeles, CA. He was the brother of John Kennedy. He was campaigning in the Democratic Party presidential primary. He was beloved by the minority community for his integrity and devotion to civil rights. RFK was perceived by many to be the only person in American politics capable of uniting its people. I didn't follow the details of the 1968 presidential election. I did know that RFK would follow in his brother's footsteps when it came to civil rights and freedom.

The summer of 1968 was a tempestuous time in American history. Both the Vietnam War and the anti-war movement were peaking. Additionally, the assassination of Martin Luther King in the spring, ignited protests and riots across the country. Chicago was heavily damaged. The decade had a tremendous influence on me, one that carved my adult path.

Moon Landing ('69)

"That's one small step for man, one giant leap for mankind." The famous words were uttered by astronaut Neil Armstrong when he planted the first human step on the moon on July 20,1969. The United States had successfully landed the first crewed mission on the moon. Apollo 11 was part of an intense effort devoted in the 1960s to be understood in the political context of its historical era. The race between the Soviet Union and the United States ended. The US claimed its rightful ownership of space dominance. [21]

My reaction to the moon landing was exuberance. The decade in which I lived was riddled with trauma—civil rights, freedom movements, liberation, Vietnam war protests, riots and human suffering. The moon landing was the most positive and exciting cultural event of the decade. It was a highlight and an accomplishment that gave Americans' hope for the future.

President ('69)

In January 1969, Richard Milhouse Nixon (RMN) became the 37th president. He had served in Congress and was Dwight Eisenhower's Vice-president. He had two notable achievements during his presidency. He ended the Vietnam War and eliminated the draft. In 1974, he resigned from office because of a scandal known as Watergate. Because I was opposed to the war and draft, Nixon's actions were welcomed with open arms. [22]

Voting Rights Act ('70)

On June 22, 1970, President Richard Nixon signed into law the lowering of the voting age to eighteen in all federal, state, and local elections. Hundreds of thousands of high school youth were eligible to vote in future elections. The time for eighteen-year-olds to vote had long been urged by young people across the United States. One of the most influential reasons was the argument that if you could die for your country, you should be allowed to vote in your country. [23]

The Act was declared unconstitutional by the Supreme Court, but less than a year later Congress passed the twenty-sixth amendment to the Constitution setting the minimum voting age to eighteen. [24]

I supported the voting right age change. I was eighteen and looked forward to exercising my voting right. My personal encounters and the influence that politics had on my life, my neighborhood and my country contributed to my opinion.

Reflection

The sixties and seventies era was a period in my life that had a significant impact on who I would become as an adult. Living in a black neighborhood, attending an all-black school, directly witnessing the struggles of the poor and blacks and the cultural influences I was exposed to during the '60s and '70s would help me contribute to making America a better place.

CHAPTER 5

TRANSITION

Early graduation from high school was an advantage. It gave me an edge on finding a job before the college kids came home for summer break. I felt relieved that I had settled my " job" situation before leaving school. I had arranged for Peter to take over for me. He had two years of high school left. The money would be helpful, but more importantly he would be safe. He was given the name "Numbers 2."

I had saved nearly three thousand dollars from my school job. I still needed to make more to get my mother, brother and two sisters out of the projects and into a house in a better neighborhood. I didn't know where to begin looking for a job. I decided to look at the employment ads in the Chicago News. Most jobs require skill and experience. I truly had no skills, and my only work experience was mowing lawns, a newspaper route, a grocery bag boy and managing the books for a gang.

Since I was good at math, I decided to try and find a job that required math and accounting skills. I found an employment ad in the Chicago Tribune, it read, "Looking for an experienced person with an accounting background." Well, I didn't have much experience, and I didn't think my work for a gang would qualify as an accounting background, but I decided to apply for the job anyway. I called the telephone number in the ad and scheduled an interview for 9 o'clock the next day.

I told my mother that I had applied for a job, and that I had an interview. She was excited for me and made sure that her alarm clock was next to my bed. I didn't sleep well that night. I worried that the only real accounting experience I had was illegal, and if I mentioned it during the interview, I wouldn't get the job, but more concerning I would end up in jail. I called the company in the morning and canceled the interview.

Back to square one. I realized that I would not find a job, if I revealed my unlawful experience, so I gave up pursuing accounting. I walked the city streets for days looking for job postings in storefronts, restaurants, and businesses. I found nothing. I had only one alternative. I called Angie and explained my situation…no job, no money. She said she would talk to her brother to see if he had work for me. Angie got back to me two days later and said her brother would like to meet me. I had never met Angie's brother during the two years I worked for him.

She arranged for us to meet that afternoon in an auto repair garage on the South Side. She gave me the address and told me to be there at two o'clock. When I got to the garage, I knocked on the door. A tall, thin, dark black man around thirty opened the rusty iron door. I noticed there were two other men standing behind him. I walked in, my mouth was bone dry, my body shook and sweat streamed down my forehead. I was told to sit.

The man who opened the door said that James would be out in a few minutes. I waited for nearly an hour. I was so scared, I thought I would pass out any minute. Finally, a short well-built black man appeared in the doorway and walked toward me. He stuck out his hand and said, "Louis, my name is James, nice to finally meet you. Angie told me about your situation, and I am grateful for the work you did for me the past two years. You helped our business grow in money and respect." James spoke.

"I may have some work for you but not the type of work you had been doing," he said. Louis asked, "What kind of work?" "I need someone to collect and bring a duffle bag to a different location every night." James said. I thought about the offer. It sounded easy but dangerous. I had no specific work skills or experience, and I realized I would not find a job that paid well. To get my mother, brother, and sisters out of the projects, I needed money. I thought, if I didn't agree, Peter's job and protection would be in jeopardy. I accepted the job and was given five collection addresses and driven to each location that night. I realized that if I were caught, I would go to jail or be killed.

The job went well for the first couple of weeks. I picked up the envelopes at each of the locations and brought them to James at the auto garage. One night, at my third pick up, no one answered the agreed upon coded knock. Instead, I heard sirens and saw flashing blue lights surrounding the house. My ride had sped away, and I was left standing in front of the house with an empty duffle bag. The police approached and asked me my name and why I was there. I gave them my name, and told them I had lost my phone and was knocking on the door to ask if I could use a phone. "What's in the bag," an officer asked? "It's empty," I said. The officer took the bag and searched its contents. It was empty. "I am not sure I believe you," said another cop. "Do you know why we are surrounding this house?" said another cop. "I have no idea," I said. The first cop said, "We have two options, one, take you to the station for questioning or two, let you use a phone." I was given a phone and called Angie. I talked to her privately, so I was able to tell her what happened. She listened and said, "Keep your mouth shut, and I will pick you up in fifteen minutes." I gave the cop his phone and told him a friend was picking me up. One patrol car stayed until Angie arrived. I thanked them and they drove off. When I got into Angie's 's car, I felt a huge sigh of relief. Angie told me she talked to her brother James and told him what happened. They agreed that I was longer a safe courier, and I was no longer useful. James gave me a pass because I had kept my mouth shut. Again, my concern was Peter. "Would Peter still be safe? I asked James, and he agreed to let him work the school job.

I was lucky I didn't end up in jail or, even worse, dead that night. I decided that a life of crime was not for me. I walked the streets for a couple weeks trying to figure out what to do about a job. I walked past DuShane high school. In the distance, I heard someone call my name.

"Hey, Louis" yelled a tall, athletic, black man. I recognized Floyd immediately. He was the high school maintenance engineer. I walked toward him, and we shook each other's hand. I had met Floyd a few times after school while waiting for Angie. He asked how I was doing. I said that I was having a hard time finding a job. "Are you still hanging out with Angie, he asked?" "No", I said. "I got into some trouble with the police and lost my job. I think it was the best thing that could have happened." I was going down the wrong path, and I knew it.

"Hanging with Angie and her brother James could only mean trouble," he said. I am sure Floyd knew I was working for them but never mentioned it. He asked, "What kind of job are you looking for?" "Well, I am good at math, and thought I might find a job as an accountant." "I am not sure, the work you were doing for James would qualify as an accountant job." Floyd said. "You're right." I spoke. I felt foolish that I had even considered applying for a job with no formal education or legitimate experience. I realized that a high school diploma was going to get me nowhere.

I thought about what I needed to do. I had three goals; one, find a job; two, help my mother; and three, get an education. I looked at Floyd and told him my plan. "I can help you with getting a job if you are interested. It's not the type of accountant job you had for the past two years, but it is in this high school," he said. "What's the job?" I asked. "We have an opening for a janitor," he spoke. At this point, I knew I couldn't be too choosy. I had to start somewhere to help my mother and to get more education. I said, "Yes, when do I start?" He told me to meet him at the school's loading dock on Monday at six o'clock. I said, "OK." Six o'clock in the morning was early for me. Nevertheless, I had a job, and I told Floyd I would be at the loading dock regardless of the time.

Monday morning arrived, and I struggled getting out of bed. Fortunately, my mother's old alarm clock worked. The alarm blared and the clock read, 5:00 AM. I showered, shaved and walked to my new job. Floyd was waiting for me on the loading dock behind the school. We went inside and discussed my hourly wage and the job responsibilities. Floyd gave me a list of work that had to be done before the school doors opened. It read, "sweep, and mop all door entries, empty hallway garbage cans, and clean all restrooms on the three floors." I was concerned that I would not have enough time to finish everything. I barely finished before students began pouring into the hallways.

I recalled the first day I entered the same doors. I never imagined that I would be the person preparing student entry for the first day of school. I walked to Floyd's office to see what he had in store for me. Floyd sat at his desk looking at a stack of papers. He lifted the first paper and read, "check the gym, pool, and outdoor bleachers for trash." I had my next assignment and walked out the door.

I knew where the gym, pool and bleachers were, so I had little trouble completing the tasks. I finished around noon just in time for lunch. My mother had made a baloney sandwich and included an apple in a brown bag. I got a cup of water and sat down to eat. Floyd rushed into the room. "No time for lunch, toilet backed up in the men's room on the third floor," he screamed. I followed him out the door and took the elevator to the third floor.

We entered the rest room and found a toilet overflowing with water, urine, and feces. We cleaned everything in an hour and took the elevator down to the basement. We no sooner got into Floyd's office and the telephone rang. It was the principal's office. The office secretary spoke, "Fight on the second floor, clean up needed." We gathered our clean up stuff and proceeded to the second floor. We found trash, blood on the walls and broken glass on the floor. We cleaned everything and went back to Floyd's office. It was four o'clock. My shift was over. What a day! I questioned whether this was the job for me. I showed up at six o'clock the next day.

When I arrived the next day, I walked the first-floor hallway checking the boy's and girl's bathrooms...all good. I smelled cigarette odors in each but no students. I walked past the trophy case near the principal's office. There were hundreds of trophies and pictures. I noticed a basketball with the inscription. "Conference Championship, 1955." Alongside of the ball was a picture of the team. Each player was named. I recognized the team captain, Floyd Weatherspoon. He was my boss. The team record was twenty one wins and two losses. I knew Floyd was an athlete but was surprised that he played ball in the same school he now works at. When I got back to his office he wasn't there. I looked around and saw several other trophies and pictures. I turned around and saw Floyd in the doorway. I questioned, "Did you play ball when you went to college?" "Yes, but I blew my knee out the first year and never played again. I stayed in college and graduated with a Mechanical Engineering degree." "How did you end up here?" I asked. "I grew up in the neighborhood and decided to stay. I married my high school sweetheart, and we agreed that we would have a family and work on the South Side. My wife is a nurse at Mercy Hospital, and we have two children. We grew up in the projects and wanted to contribute to making the neighborhood a better place." It became clear to me that Floyd gave me a job, because he saw that I was floundering and had the potential to make something out of myself. Idecided not to disappoint him.

Summer ('68)

I continued to work as a janitor and Floyd taught me how to fix boilers, repair plumbing and troubleshoot electrical problems. I had a knack for the work, but knew I wanted to follow a different path. I was interested in helping other kids like me, who may mix with the wrong crowd or be lured into a gang.

I investigated community college catalogs and found a program titled, Human Services. I had no idea what it meant. I showed the catalog to Floyd, and he explained what it meant and how I could use the degree to help kids like me. A year passed, and I was still on the job. Floyd was patient with me, and he encouraged me to pursue my interest. I was grateful for all that Floyd did. He had become my mentor. While working, I checked on Peter periodically to make sure he was safe. I knew I had to help him finish school and break ties with James.

During the year, I saved more money. I had five thousand dollars. Was it enough to buy a car? I knew that if I wanted to go to school, I would need transportation. I was probably the only eighteen year old in Chicago that didn't have a driver's license. I made an appointment to get my license and for three months Floyd taught me how to drive. I used his car and passed the road test. I was set…time to go shopping. I had never owned a car and didn't know where to begin. I talked to Floyd and asked for his help. There were plenty of car dealers in the neighborhood. Floyd took me to a friend's car lot. There were rows and rows of used cars for sale. I decided to spend five hundred dollars. Floyd's friend said, "That's all? An older car is the best I can do." He showed me a '57 Ford. It was orange and white and looked good to me.

Floyd asked about its history, looked under the hood, checked the tires, exhaust and oil pan. He asked the car dealer to start her up. She roared like a lion! We took it for a ride, and I decided that the car was the best I could do for the money. We drove off the lot and headed toward Floyd's house. I dropped him off at his house and drove to the projects. I parked in the designated lot for our building, locked the doors and hurried excitedly to our apartment. I unlocked the door and yelled to my mother, brother, and sisters, "Who wants to go for a ride in my car and get ice cream?" They all screamed at one time, "I do."

I checked the community college catalog to see when the next semester would start. Enrollment ended on September 1st. It was August 28th. I filled out the application that came with the catalog, mailed it and hoped for the best. I received a letter from the college three days later. I was accepted and learned that the Human Services program would begin on September 15th. My course schedule was included in the letter. I was excited but nervous.

I went to Floyd's office to tell him the good news. All the courses were in night school so there was no conflict with my work schedule. Floyd was excited for me and wished me the best.

I had two classes each evening on Tuesday and Thursday. My first class was titled, "An Introduction to Human Services" and the second class was "Introduction to Psychology." I got home that evening and couldn't believe I was going to college and starting a career to help neighborhood kids. I completed my first semester and got two B's. I promised myself that next semester my grades would be A's.

'69 - '70

I continued working with Floyd and attended night classes that year. My '57 Ford got me back and forth to work and school. All was going well. I had saved a little more money, and I hoped that by next year I would have enough money to buy my mother a house. But everything changed one cold winter night while driving from school to home. My car skid on black ice, and I lost control. I wasn't hurt, but my car was. I ditched the car in a ravine and had to walk to a nearby store. I called a tow truck company, and my car was pulled out and brought to a repair garage. The cost for the tow and repairs was three hundred dollars. I dug into my meager savings. What a setback! I took a bus to night school and Floyd brought me back and forth to work. When the two weeks ended, I was back on the road again and motivated to complete another year of college. I figured at this pace, I would complete the community college Human Services Program in four years.

The national and local cultural influences between 1960 and 1970 had an impact on the direction my life would take. The Hippie counterrevolution, Vietnam War, and civil rights issues haunted me. I felt a need to jump in and make a contribution to reversing the universal inequities and racial discrimination that existed throughout the US, but more importantly, the negative influence the movements had on Chicago.

Living in the South Side projects and going to a predominantly all black school sensitized me to the plight of the poor. I thought about my first step. Do I want to align myself with a political party, activist group, or go it alone? I observed a couple of groups at college protesting the need for a more diverse curriculum. One that included courses in black history and the current contemporary urban concerns like improved housing conditions and school integration.

I decided to learn more about the college activists. The protesters handed out leaflets that advertised a meeting at the college center on Thursday evening at 8 o'clock. I decided to attend. I got to the meeting just as it started. The group leader was speaking about the process of introducing black history courses to the Human Services curriculum. Her words piqued my interest immediately. I met with the speaker after the meeting. Her name was Maria. She was in her second year and matriculating in the same program as mine. I introduced myself and told her about my interest in helping the poor. We connected within minutes and began talking about helping one another.

My concern was more aligned with the racial discrimination of the blacks in my neighborhood. I wanted to help improve the education of poor kids. I asked Maria if she would help. She said, "I will give it some thought and let you know." The following week, I met Maria in the school cafeteria and asked if she had made a decision about helping me. She answered "Yes." We started sharing our thoughts and ideas. We made a plan to devote time to helping black and poor white children attending segregated schools.

Maria had attended mostly all-white schools from elementary through high school. She had little contact with blacks and poor whites. However, she was a passionate supporter of school integration and understood the benefits of its practice both for blacks and poor whites. We understood that if black and poor white students had the opportunity to attend white schools the inequalities that existed would decrease. Black and poor white children living in the inner city neighborhoods would have the advantage of better buildings, better curricula, and other resources like certified teachers, trained counselors, and more supplies and materials. My school situation was a good example. I lived in the projects. I attended a black school. I had no other options.

To start, we investigated the current situation in the Chicago city schools. We found that beginning in 1970, the white portion of the school population fell nearly 75 percent, despite some halfhearted efforts in the '60s. Chicago never developed an exchange program between suburban and city schools. Suburban schools remained largely segregated as well.

Forced bussing to segregate public schools in Chicago was implemented in the 1971 school year and extended to 1980. The percentage of blacks attending mostly-minority schools decreased from 66.9 percent to 62.9 percent. The decrease was not significant, but the result was a downward trend to build on. In the early 1970s, there was a court-ordered desegregation plan, but there were a few white students left in the system. This made meaningful desegregation almost impossible across the city's public school system. [24]

Our effort was in vain. The system had repeated itself over time, and school integration did not look promising. My personal experience wasn't enough to take on a broken system at this time. Possibly things would change, and a stronger and more concerted effort would take place.

Maria and I remained friends for the next few years. We hung out when we could and compared "notes" on our concerns and heartfelt interests. She was a great friend!

'68 - '70

It had been two years since high school graduation and starting my job with Floyd. I had completed four college courses and still had a long way to go before getting my Human Services degree.

My family situation had not improved. My mother and sisters were stuck in the projects and Peter had lost protection because he had graduated. I had nearly seven thousand dollars saved but was unsure if it was enough to put a down payment on a house. My mother had worked extremely hard the past couple of years to the point that she was exhausted. I was very concerned about her health and strength to care for my siblings. Peter was looking for a job but was not successful. Something had to give. I decided to look for a new house and another job. I would put college on hold for a while.

I knew nothing about buying a house or where to begin. My only option was to talk to Floyd. My first question was, "Where?" I realized that a house in Hyde Park was out of question but an apartment might be a possibility. Floyd and I looked for apartments that my mother and I could afford. We figured with her income and my savings we could afford three hundred dollars a month. Our first attempt was futile. Most apartments we looked at were out of our price range. We decided that a Hyde Park apartment was unrealistic. We eventually found a two-bedroom apartment above a deli in the Englewood area. The apartment wasn't the best, but we would be out of the projects and living in a neighborhood that was less dangerous and had more community and school diversity.

We were excited about moving to our new home. My mother appreciated how hard I had worked to make it happen. My brother, Peter, had a better chance for success, and my two sisters would start junior high without fear and an opportunity to get a better education. I was pleased that we moved, and proud that I was able to help my family. It was time to find a second job.

I heard about an afternoon cleaning job in a nearby school. The school was within walking distance from our new home. I decided to check it out after work. The school was very small and did not resemble what I had imagined. I approached the front door and rang the doorbell. Within minutes, a tall blonde woman approached. "Hi," I said. "My name is Louis and a friend told me about a possible job." "Yes, my name is Sheila, come in," she said. The building had one floor, ten classrooms and a couple of offices. I asked,

“Is this a school?” “Yes, but not like a traditional school” she said, “It is an Alternative Education Program for teens who are at risk,” Sheila offered. “At risk of what?” I asked. “They are kids who have broken laws, belong to gangs and are unable to function in a large school setting. They have the desire to succeed, but need individual attention and academic support.” I wasn’t familiar with this type of school but thought it certainly was needed.

Sheila told me that there was an opening for a person to clean the building for four hours Monday through Friday. She showed me around and described the responsibilities. I told her about my current job, gave her my contact information and used Floyd as a reference. She wrote down the information and told me she would call when she made a decision. I waited for a few days and Sheila called. She offered the job to me, and I accepted. She asked, “Can you start on Monday at four o’clock?” I responded, “Yes, see you then.”

Our new neighborhood, Englewood, was a lot different from the Fuller Park area. We no longer lived in an apartment in a nineteen-story building with hundreds of poor people. It was a drastic change. It was like night and day compared to living in the projects. Living above a deli was different. We had immediate access to groceries and other household needs. We were within walking distance to stores, restaurants, and schools. Our location was an advantage for my family. The area was much safer than living in the projects; there were literally no problems or concerns with gangs or other tenants. Our new location was safer than the Fuller Park arca, which was known for repeated crime, violence, and murders. Although our life had improved markedly, I wanted to eventually find a house for my mother.

I arrived at my new job at exactly four o’clock. Sheila met me at the door and escorted me to a supply room next to the cafeteria. She showed me where the cleaning supplies, mops and brooms were located. There were ten classrooms, three offices, a cafeteria and gym to clean every night. I finished the first day’s work within thirty minutes to spare. Shelia arrived at eight o’clock to check my work. She was pleased.

When I arrived at work the next day, I walked straight to the supply room to gather the supplies and things needed to start work. I walked by one of the classrooms and heard Sheila talking to one of the kids. She spoke to him in a very calm and assertive tone. She explained that his behavior was not appropriate and as a consequence he would work with me for the remainder of the week. She noticed me walking by the office and asked me to come in. She explained the situation and introduced me to Matt. We walked to the first classroom, and I told Matt what we had to do. He worked well without saying a word the entire four hours.

The following day, I met Matt in the supply room. He was ready to work. He still hadn't said a word to me. I decided to break the ice. "Matt, do you live near this school?" He said nothing as we walked to the next classroom. He finally opened up and said, "No, I live in the Fuller Park area. "How do you get to school," I asked. He said he takes a city bus to the Edgewood school. I knew that could take almost an hour. I told him that I had lived in the projects for two years. He gave me a surprised look. I told him my story. He asked a few questions and seemed to warm up to me. We finished our work for the day and walked out the front door. I asked. "Do you want a ride home? Where do you live in Fuller Park?" Matt said, "I live in the Robert Taylor Housing projects. I told him that I knew exactly where the projects were located. The projects were my home for two years.

Matt accepted the ride. During the thirty-minute drive, he filled me in on his struggles and dreams. As we approached the projects, flashbacks entered my mind. I thought about our apartment, the constant noise inside and outside the building and the nightly blaring sirens and flashing blue lights. I recalled my illegal school job, my protection plan for Peter and me, and my goal to get my mother out of the horrible environment. Matt got out of the car and slammed the door. The noise broke my trance. He said, "Good night and thank you." I sped away from the curb anxious to get back to the Edgewood neighborhood.

Matt finished working with me on Friday. I thanked him for his help and asked if he would agree to hang out sometime. He said, "Yes." I empathized with Matt and recognized that his life paralleled mine. He grew up in a better neighborhood and was forced to move to the projects because his father had left his mother and two siblings with no financial support or a place to live. He had been living in the projects for three years. He did well in school but decided to drop out. A school counselor told him about the alternative program, and he applied and was accepted. He was in his second year and needed another year to complete the graduation requirements.

I thought about Floyd and his valued support. He gave me a job, encouraged me to go to college and helped our family find a better place to live. He was truly a friend, and the reason I got back on a positive track.

I thought a lot about Matt and whether or not I could help him overcome his personal issues. I wasn't sure if Sheila would agree with my plan. When I got to work on Monday, I asked Sheila if we could talk about my helping Matt. She said, "I don't think that would be a good idea. First of all, Matt needs adult support not a friend. Second, his needs are being supported with counseling," Sheila said "He is dealing with a couple of sensitive issues and the timing might not be right. I suggest that you wait a couple of months and then approach him about doing an activity together." I appreciated Shelia's recommendation and planned on waiting until Matt was in a better place. That never happened. Matt quit school, joined a gang, and ended up in a juvenile detention center. He was just sixteen and headed toward a life of uncertainty. I often thought about him. Maybe, our paths would cross again someday.

I continued working two jobs, saving money, and preparing for my return to school. My mother and siblings had settled into our new life. My mother continued working at the meat packing plant, and Peter decided to get a job and save for school. My two sisters adjusted well to their new school and were happy about our new home and neighborhood. I was pleased with the direction my life was taking and looking forward to my future.

'72

I was approaching my 22nd birthday and anxious to register for the fall semester. I was driving home from my afternoon job and noticed that the traffic ahead of me had slowed to a crawl. Two ambulances, sirens screeching and lights blinking passed my car. I was certain that there was an accident a couple blocks away. As I approached the scene, I saw two cars tangled together and two bodies lying next to them. As I approached the cars, I glanced quickly at the bodies and thought I recognized one. She looked like Maria! I drove past and parked my car in a vacant lot. I ran to the scene. Of course, I was stopped by yellow tape and a blue uniform. I wasn't sure if it was Maria, but I had to find out.

Two EMTs placed Maria on a gurney and wheeled her to a waiting ambulance. My only option was to follow the ambulance to the hospital. When I arrived, she had been taken to the emergency room. I rushed in and inquired about the accident victim. The nurse asked, "Are you a relative?" I told her that I wasn't, but the victim might be a friend. I asked, "Can you tell me her name?" "That is confidential unless you are a relative," she answered. I told her that if she were my friend, she had no relatives. She was reluctant but told me her first name was Maria.

My heart pounded rapidly and tears trickled down my cheeks. "Thank you," I said. I waited until morning, hoping I could find out if she was okay. I approached the nurse's station and told the supervisor that I was checking on Maria. The nurse asked, "Are you a relative?" I said, "No, but I am a good friend." She didn't give me much information, but told me she had been moved to a room and was in critical condition. I knew Maria didn't have any family in Chicago and was working and putting herself through college on her own. I was unable to see her that morning. I went to my day job and told Floyd about the accident. He recommended I try to see her in the evening. I finished my second job at eight o'clock and hurried to the hospital before visiting hours ended. I inquired at the nurse's desk. Still unable to get much information, I was told that Maria was still in critical condition, and that she may improve within a couple days. I visited the following three days. There was no change.

On the fourth day, I was told that Maria was responding to the care and was given the "serious" condition label. On the fifth day, Maria's condition had improved, and visitors were permitted. I was given her room number, approached her door and knocked gently. A familiar voice said, "Come in." She was surprised and happy to see me. We talked for a while until her eyes could no longer remain open. I walked out the door pleased that I had finally seen her and hopeful she would continue her recovery.

I visited Maria the next couple of weeks until she was well enough to return to her apartment. The day she was dismissed, I drove her home from the hospital and helped her settle. She was healthy enough to take care of herself but would need help with groceries and household care. A month passed and Maria was fully mended. The fall semester had begun. We were both excited to return to the Human Services program.

The teacher aide job in the Alternative Education Program gave me an opportunity to observe teachers in action. Although most of the classes were held during the day, there were opportunities to witness the interaction and strategies that teachers used to motivate students, The human service courses I was taking gave me insight into the psychological and emotional needs that many of the students possessed. After working with Floyd for four years and working as a teacher aide, I realized that my career path was helping others. My experiences in the projects and DuSable High School gave me the motivation to work with disadvantaged youth.

CHAPTER 6
CAREER DECISION

I worked with Floyd for four years and at the alternative school for a year. I recognized that my career goal was not school maintenance or clean up. I was thankful for Floyd's guidance and support and for Sheila's willingness to give me a part-time janitor job. I knew that to reach my goal to help kids, I needed to finish the Human Services program.

A requirement for the Human Services program was a three-month internship. I decided to ask Shelia if she would agree to sponsoring my internship in the at-risk program. I met with Sheila and discussed my idea with her. She said, "The program could use a teacher's aide." We agreed that I would work as an aide from twelve to four o'clock and continue with my janitor job from four to eight o'clock. There was just one glitch. I had a full-time job working with Floyd. The next day, I sat down with Floyd to discuss my plan. He agreed to a morning part-time position. Everything was set, and I started my career path the following week. I realized how fortunate I was to secure the internship and continue to work at both schools.

My position was titled "teacher aide." I was assigned to a classroom working with Mrs. Bea. I had walked by her classroom while doing my cleaning job and recognized that her commitment was authentic. She was a no-nonsense and committed teacher. I was excited about my assignment with her.

My first day as an aide, I walked into Mrs. Bea's classroom with anxiety and trepidation. What had I gotten myself into? Mrs. Bea introduced me to the ten-member class. She told them that I would be helping her and them for three months. My first assignment was to escort the students to gym class and stay with them until the class ended.

When the class was finished, I brought the group back to the classroom. Mrs. Bea was waiting and had prepared an English grammar lesson. I sat in the back of the classroom observing her teaching methods and the students' acceptance of the content. I was impressed with Mrs. Bea's instructional approach and student participation. I asked myself, "Could I be a good teacher?"

I continued working my two part-time jobs for three months. During that time, I learned a lot and connected with a few of the students. Most of them struggled in traditional school and brought a lot of behavioral and emotional baggage to the program. I identified with their needs and often shared my story. I was accepted and felt that helped. As I gained more confidence, I knew that my chosen career would follow a path connected to disadvantaged youth.

I walked into the classroom one afternoon and sensed that something was wrong. The kids seemed sad and just not acting normally. Mrs. Bea was sitting at her desk talking to one of the students. She got up from her chair and walked toward me. "Louis," she asked, "would you mind stepping into the hallway for a minute?" She told me that Allen, one the students had attempted suicide and overdosed on heroin. He was hospitalized and not expected to live. She said the students were distraught and class was cancelled. They would be dismissed shortly and bused home. I walked back into the classroom and waited for dismissal. I had talked to Allen several times and knew of his struggles. I was surprised that he would attempt suicide but understood how situations become unmanageable and taking one's life becomes the only option.

Allen died the next day. Mrs. Bea, Shelia, the students, and I attended the funeral. His classmates were traumatized and visibly shaken. We tried to console them and deal with their feelings. Allen was well-liked by his peers and would be missed by all. The kids struggled for the next few days but with counseling and the support of Mrs. Bea and Shelia they were able to overcome their sorrow. Shelia arranged for counselors to help the students manage their grief.

Allen's death affected me as well. I experienced peer death while living in the projects and while attending high school in Fuller Park. During the two years I lived there, three kids died from overdoses and two committed suicide. My resolution to help teens was reinforced, and I made a commitment that I would dedicate my life to making an impact on needy youth.

I finished my internship in three months and resumed my full- and part-time jobs. I was officially designated a sophomore in the two-year program. I figured it would take two more years to get my Associate Degree. I continued to save money to pay for a bachelor's degree and to pursue the goal of returning my mother to Hyde Park.

CHAPTER 7

UNEXPECTED INVITATION

It was the end of the school day, and I was on my way to the cafeteria to mop the floors and take the trash to the dumpster. The principal, Mr. Roberts, walked in and said, "Hello Louis." I responded, "Hi." I met the principal the first week I started the job at DuSable High School. Most of the staff and students called him Mr. R. He was well respected by the teachers and staff. Students often commented that he was tough but fair. He told me that he had been keeping track of my work and college pursuits. He mentioned that he was proud of my accomplishments, and that I had become a positive role model for several students. I thought if he only knew the true story.

Mr. Roberts asked if I would be interested in speaking to the graduating seniors at the June commencement. I was surprised and shocked at the same time. I didn't think anyone other than Floyd knew about my experiences since graduation. "That's it" I thought. Floyd had been giving him information about me. I asked, "Did Floyd share my story with you?" He responded, "Yes, what do you think about speaking to the students at the graduation ceremony?" "I said, I had never spoken to a small or large group. I don't even know what I would say." He suggested that I tell the students about my work and educational pursuits for the last four years. He said my experiences would be motivating and inspirational.

The graduation was one month away. I didn't know if I could prepare a speech with such short notice, but more importantly, could I even give it. When I got home that evening, I told my mother about the invitation. She wasn't surprised. She knew how hard I had devoted my time and energy to work and school. She was proud of me and wanted my brother and sisters to follow in my footsteps.

Two days later, I approached Mr. Roberts, and told him that I would speak at the ceremony. He was elated and told me if I needed help with my speech to let him know. I sat down at the kitchen table a few days later and began to jot down what I had experienced since high school graduation. I started with my job at DuSable High School, my mentorship with Floyd, my pursuit of a degree in Human Services, a friend's car accident, my internship at the alternative program, the suicide death of one of the students, and my future goals. I hoped that the kids would respond positively and not "boo" me out of the auditorium.

The month passed by quickly. I had bought a new suit, shirt, and tie for the occasion. I didn't go to work that afternoon. I got home from work around four thirty. I rehearsed my speech at least ten times. I was too nervous to eat and paced around the apartment before heading to the graduation. I noticed that my mother and siblings were not in the apartment. I walked out of the apartment door, speech in hand and drove to DuSable High School. When I got there, I met with Mr. Roberts. He asked, "Are you ready?" I responded, "As ready as I can be." He introduced me to the graduating seniors and told them why he had chosen me to be the commencement speaker.

I was extremely nervous and trembling a lot. I walked to the podium and looked out at the students. There were more than five hundred eyes staring at me. I looked down at the front row and there sat my mother, brother, sisters, Floyd and his family, Sheila, and Maria. I was in shock.

The time had come to make a fool of myself. I began with thanking Mr. Roberts for his confidence in me and his belief that my experiences could influence the graduates. I pulled my speech out of my suit coat pocket and began to speak. The first couple of words that came out of my mouth were strained, and I'm sure unintelligible. I started with my job at DuSable and ended with my future goals. The speech took about five minutes. It seemed like an hour. When I finished, the students, my family and friends stood and clapped loudly. I was happy that the speech was over and I was thrilled with the applause.

Interlude One

Latisha peered through the living room doorway trying not to be noticed. Even though I was writing my novel, any slight movement or distraction would catch my eye. I usually watched TV while writing and concentrated more on my laptop keys than a sporting event, movie or weekly series displayed on the screen.

She interrupted my thought process and asked, "How's it going?" I answered, "It's going." I realized when writing a novel there is no gauge to measure progress or accuracy. It was hit or miss. I decided to give Latisha an abridged accounting of my book status.

I began with the *prologue.* I told her that the story was introduced with the discussion that we had about writing my life story. The synopsis included mention of my imaginary porch visitor and my inquiry about the value of my life story to potential readers. I told her that her encouragement had motivated me to tell my story, and I had decided to move forward.

"How much have you completed," she asked? I responded, "I've written sixty-one pages and twenty thousand words. I read that the average number of pages for a novel is two hundred fifty pages and ninety thousand words." "I have miles to go before I sleep."

Latisha listened intently as I explained each chapter. She knew I had written intermittently for a month but knew nothing about the seven chapters I had completed. I told her the introductory chapter included an identification of ten secrets to writing a book, the importance of having a good idea, deciding on the genre, the need for a plot line, and the inclusion of literary devices. I added that I also decided to identify chapters with a timeline. The strategy would chart my life story and help readers move through a seventy-year period more easily, I told her that I came up with the technique and named it "recall."

On occasion, when reading, I often refreshed my memory of dates and events by backtracking. I would thumb through chapters searching for information. The recall technique was used in several chapters and above paragraphs to identify dates. I hoped that this practice would provide story continuity. Latisha liked the recall technique because she also had difficulty remembering dates and events in books that extended for many years.

I identified the titles of the remaining six chapters for her: Chapter 2, Early Years; Chapter 3, High School; Chapter 4, Cultural Influences; Chapter 5, Transition; Chapter 6, Career Decisions; and Chapter 7, Unexpected Event. Latisha asked, "Where did you get all that information for each chapter?" I told her, "Most of the information was obtained from Google and Wikipedia." I decided to wait until I finished the book to reveal more details. Latisha was impressed with my progress and looked forward to the next update.

PART II

CHAPTER 8

GRADUATION

The next two years flew by. I worked both jobs and went to school part time. I had two more courses to take before I graduated. I was pleased with my accomplishments and looked forward to finding a job that complements a Human Services Degree.

I had taken a couple of psychology courses and thought I might like to counsel teens. I found out that two courses in psychology did not qualify for a counseling position. I needed a Bachelor of Arts degree. I thought about teaching and realized a teacher's certificate was needed with a concentration in a specific subject area. I became discouraged and thought that my associate degree was worthless.

I recalled my internship at the alternative school. I enjoyed working with Mrs. Bea and Shelia. I saw them occasionally while working at the school. I thought about Allen's death and how it affected his friends and me. I identified with his struggles and the needs of others his age. I questioned whether I would be a good fit as a teacher aide. I decided that I would approach Shelia about a job the next time I saw her.

It was two weeks before graduation, and I hadn't talked to Shelia about a job. I didn't feel confident about my coursework or experiences. One day I saw her walk into her office and decided the timing was right. I knocked on her door and she said, "Come in. How are you Louis"? I said, "Fine." "How can I help you, she asked?" I told her I was graduating in two weeks with an Associate Degree in Human Services. "Yes, I recall, you were working toward the degree when you interned with us." "I thought that the internship experience and my course work might qualify for a teacher aide position," I spoke. She said, "based on that internship and your commencement speech, I think you are more than qualified. However, we don't have an opening right now. I will keep you in mind for an interview if a position opens," she spoke. "Thank you," I responded. "By the way, would you like to attend my graduation?" I asked. "I certainly would, please send the details to me," she said. I was pleased with my conversation with Sheila and hoped an opening would become available. I finished my work and thought about my conversation on the way home. I felt better about my degree and the possibility of working at the Alternative Education Program.

Graduation night arrived. I was one of fifty-five graduates who had completed all the requirements for the Human Services Degree. Maria was one of them. We were proud of our accomplishments and the support we gave each other. Our names were called individually and when we reached the podium, diplomas were placed in our hands. The six-year effort had paid off, and I was now the proud owner of an associate degree. The class of 1974 threw their mortarboards in unisons toward the sky...recognizing that the sky was the limit.

My mother had arranged a graduation party at a church hall. The deli owner who owned the shop below our apartment provided the food and drinks, my sister oversaw the music and had secured a local teen band. Peter gave a Pepsi toast and a congratulatory speech. With tears in his eyes, he expressed his pride for me, my accomplishments and all that I had done for him. A tear trickled down my cheeks.

As the party was ending, Shelia approached and congratulated me. She spoke, "I have a graduation present for you. A teacher aide position opened, and I am offering it to you." I was thrilled. I uttered, "I accept." "The full-time position begins on Monday; will that be a problem? I know you currently have two jobs," she remarked. "I don't think so," I responded. "I can find a replacement for you," she said. I looked for Floyd and told him the good news. He was elated and said he had a replacement who could begin on Monday. I thanked him, told my mother the good news and walked out of the church hall beaming with pride about my new job and future.

CHAPTER 9

NURTURE VERSUS NATURE

The tumultuous sixties had passed and my life for the first few years of the seventies was challenging but rewarding. Key personal issues and events that had influenced my growth and development were my father's death, our move to the projects, a new high school experience, my first job and earning a two-year associate degree. Worldly influences included the assassinations of JFK. MLK and RFK, the Vietnam War, the Civil Rights Movement, the Hippie counterrevolution and education reform.

I suspected that both personal and worldly events influenced my attitude, opinions and the direction my adult life would take. I questioned...do life experiences and the environment (nurture) or genetics (nature) play a greater role in determining behavioral traits and characteristics? Are resiliency characteristics like the strength and resolve to overcome setbacks, tragedies, barriers learned or inherited? Both questions are debatable and have gone unanswered for hundreds of years.

I believed that a strong family unit, positive neighborhood experiences, morals learned in church and values and ethics reinforced by my parents influenced my belief system. I recognized that my father and mother's work ethic, willingness to help others and moral code are behavioral characteristics that I possess. I also believed that I had inherited behavioral traits like commitment, resolve and the strength to overcome adversities.

The degree or percentage to which the environment or genetics contributed to the growth and development of my behavioral characteristics and traits is unknown. I believed that both nurture and nature contributed to whom I had become and would have a future impact on my education and career choices.

The two psychology courses I had taken in the Human Services Program were interesting and enlightening but didn't answer the age-old theory question...nature or nurture? Was human behavior influenced by the environment or were humans born with a genetic structure and hard-wired for right or wrong, good, or bad, weak or strong, liberal or conservative, or prejudiced or not?

I had learned that several behavioral scientists supported the theory that human behavior was either one hundred percent environmental or one hundred percent genetic. Some theorists answered the question with a majority or minority percentage...like sixty percent environment and forty percent genetic.

I believed that personal behavioral characteristics like sensitivity and concern for the poor influenced my political ideology, commitment to civil rights, opposition to the Vietnam war, the need for school reform, and the integration of schools were influenced by my environment. Also, living in the projects, attending a segregated school, and having menial work experiences influenced my political views. I had developed an opinion that politicians made decisions based on the premise that "the end justifies the means."

I had recognized that my political opinions and beliefs were influenced by the political decisions that disregarded the plight of blacks and poor whites. I believed that politicians were more concerned with reelection, compensation/benefits, a desire for power, a commitment to maintaining political party control and the spread of a preferred ideology.

Politicians often opposed policies and programs that would reduce poverty, improve housing, provide healthcare for all and impose school reform. Ineffective federal, state, and local legislation and lack of commitment continued to plague Chicago and the South Side during my teens and adult life.

Political decisions like the US involvement in the Vietnam War was a tragedy that should have never happened. The fifteen-year war took the lives of more than fifty-eight thousand soldiers and more than seventy-five thousand returned from the war with Post Traumatic Disorder Syndrome (PTSD). Thousands of veterans returned home without jobs, with no education, and with negative reactions from protesters. [25]

The toll of the war was immeasurable. It affected individuals and families whether black or white, rich or poor or living in a city, suburbia or the country. The loss of family, friends and the unknown haunted me. War scars never heal and are branded in the hearts of many people for life.

Other cultural issues and events that took place during the sixties and seventies included the hippie counterculture movement. It encompassed all that I believed. The movement's generational stand on the Vietnam War, liberalism, freedom of expression and peaceful protest had a measurable impact on me. I became a free thinker, opinionated, and committed to causes I passionately believed. I was vehemently opposed to the war, to negative opinions about returning veterans and to destructive and violent protests. I carried these beliefs into adulthood and tried to use them in my personal and career decisions.

Another significant environmental influence was our family's move to the projects and the change in high schools. The living conditions were a drastic change, and the high school was significantly different in respect to diversity, integration/segregation, curriculum choice, teacher certification, and building disrepair and neglect.

I learned from firsthand experience that housing and school reform were a must. I witnessed racial discrimination, prejudice and bias from politicians, school administrators and teachers. The disproportionate percentage of black and white kids attending schools was disconcerting. I recognized that racial balance among schools could be achieved by busing a percentage of white kids to black schools and a percentage of black kids to white schools. The issue was a no-brainer, but politicians, school boards and parents often could not see the benefit. The customary response to improvements for people living in poverty was a dollar issue. At the time, I recognized that if money was spent wisely, in the long run the economic return would help all Americans. This political short sightedness was quite obvious to me.

In retrospect, I benefited from living and going to school in two distinctly different environments. My experiences and exposure to two different environments (nurture) growing up in Hyde Park and Fuller Park helped me mature, gave me a belief system and a path for my future personal and career life.

CHAPTER 10

CAREER PATH

I rose early Monday morning anxious to begin my new job. It was an unusually chilly September day, but the sun shone brightly, and I anticipated my teacher aide position would offer an opportunity to help struggling teens.

Sheila had assigned me to Mr. Sikorski's classroom. He was middle-aged, short. stocky and balding. He was recognized as an excellent math teacher. He welcomed me to Room 152. I hoped that it would be my home for several years.

Mr. S. asked me to take a seat to discuss his teaching methods and to review my responsibilities before the students arrived. He explained that he taught five math classes a day—two junior high and three high school courses. Sheila had told him I was good at math. I suspected that was the reason I was assigned to him.

He explained that there were two important methods he used to teach at-risk students. One, assure the students that he knew the content. That is, "what" to teach. Second, and more important, "how" to teach. He explained that at-risk students often come from broken homes, are raised without fathers, drug influenced, gang threatened and below grade level in reading and math. He said that many of the students had social, emotional, and psychological problems that prevented them from learning and controlling their behavior. Mr. S. was about to offer more insight just as the students started to enter the room. He said, "Let's continue our conversation later." I nodded, okay. I felt fortunate to have the opportunity to work with Mr. S.

Nine students came into the classroom and sat in the empty chairs. Mr. S. greeted them and asked their names. He assigned them to seats alphabetically. I asked him later, "Why?" He said, "Assigned seating separates friends from friends." I thought if Mr. S. was that insightful, I'm going to learn a lot.

I observed Mr. S. teach each of the five classes from a seat in the back of the room. None of the students spoke to me nor did Mr. S. throughout the day. At the end the day, Mr. S asked me to sit with him. He asked, "What did you observe about the students in each of the five classes?" I thought about the question for a few minutes and struggled with giving him an answer. Fortunately, I had taken notes about the classes. I said, "Each of the classes was different. Students in the junior high classes concentrated less and didn't have a good math foundation. The older students seemed more interested and had more skills." "Excellent, you were very observant," he spoke. He explained, "The reason for the difference between the younger and older students was maturation and confidence. The junior high students were still acquiring responsibility and learning skills to build confidence." Of course, I realized that other environmental factors may impact their maturity and confidence.

We continued our conversation for another hour. Mr. S. wanted to learn more about me and what my career goals were. I told him about living in the Hyde Park and the Fuller Park areas. I described how living on both "sides of the track" gave me a perspective that most teens did not have. I explained that I wanted to use that experience to help disadvantaged youth either in a school setting or social service capacity. He applauded my interest and pledged he would help me achieve my goals.

Within a few days, my teacher aide role and responsibilities were more defined. I began helping students in the classroom with math concepts and problems. I identified more with the younger kids, probably because older students were learning higher math skills. I also enjoyed their energy and spontaneity.

After working with Mr. S. for a month, I learned a lot and felt comfortable with both student groups. I had told some of the students about my teen years growing up in two distinctly different environments, attending a predominantly black high school and my interest in helping teens. I thought that my honesty and story helped me connect with many of them. I had gained the trust of some, and they began to share personal issues with me. I shared my progress with Mr. S from time to time, and he advised that I should not get too close or involved with their personal lives. I understood the reason for his recommendation and adhered to it.

The first year as an aide flew by quickly. I continued to learn from Mr. S and began to achieve my goal of helping young people. I acquired some teaching skills and a greater understanding of teens and their struggles. I realized that my teen story was minor compared to the stories students often shared with me.

During the summer months, I resumed my janitorial responsibilities at the Alternative Education program, I can honestly say that mopping floors, cleaning toilets, and unloading trucks we're not high on my enjoyment list. I looked forward to the beginning of the new school year, working with Mr. S. and helping students.

The first day of school arrived, and I was anxious to meet the new kids. The first junior high group filed in, and Mr. S. assigned them seats alphabetically. There were six boys and five girls. They were all new faces to me except one of the boys. For some reason, he looked familiar.

The class lasted forty-five minutes and during that time none of the students spoke. They just listened. The boy who looked familiar was named Jimmy. I watched him during the class and tried to recall where I had seen him. The class was dismissed, and I followed the students out the door. Jimmy headed for the boy's room, and I followed. I opened the door and was hit with a blast of smoke. There was another boy in the room with Jimmy. He was puffing on a cigarette and looked straight at me as he exhaled a puff of smoke. I looked at both and told them to put the cigarettes out and to follow me. They complied and I took them to Shelia's office. I explained what happened, and she took over.

The next day, I looked for Jimmy in the first period class. He wasn't there. I asked Sheila where Jimmy was, and she said that she suspended him, and he chose to quit school. "He was a court ordered placement and that one infraction of school rules would mean a return to a delinquent youth center." That was the last time I saw him. I thought about Jimmy occasionally and wondered why he looked so familiar.

The day-to-day responsibilities of my teacher aide job were challenging and rewarding. It was difficult at times to get the students motivated. Mr. S assigned a couple of students to me whom I helped during study hall. Both were junior high age and lacked math foundation skills like multiplication tables and fraction concepts. I worked with them every day for three months. At times, I wasn't sure I helped. One day, I asked Matt, "Can you tell me the multiples of nine?"He responded immediately and correctly. I was surprised and felt successful.

There were a few students who came to school each day without lunch, with dirty clothes and half asleep. I imagined their home situations and how they influenced their behaviors and learning. I realized that I enjoyed helping students with math, but recognized that I wanted to offer more support. A teacher's job is difficult at times but inspiring when students learn. I had a desire to know more about a student's personal life and help accordingly. I decided that I would return to school and earn a bachelor's degree in counseling or social work.

CHAPTER 11

GOALS ACHIEVED

My mother, brother, sisters and I had been living in the Englewood apartment for three years. My mother continued to work in the meat packing plant and Peter attended night classes and earned a certificate in computer repair. My two sisters had completed junior high and were in their first year of high school. My '57 Ford broke down on my way to work, so I bought a ten-year-old Chevy. My first set of "wheels" had been good to me. The miles logged helped me get to my first full-time job and a two-year college degree. I set out on accomplishing my next goal...a house for my mother.

I had saved enough money for a down payment on a house in the Hyde Park area that I had left five years ago, and I wanted to return to the place where I had lived for sixteen years. I realized that we couldn't afford a large house. My mother and I searched the area for two months and finally found a suitable house.

The house had a small front porch, the number of bedrooms needed, and positioned on a tree-lined street. We left our apartment in Englewood and joyfully moved into our new home. We had overcome the hardships of living in the projects and attending schools that had limited resources.

My goal to find a house for my mother was achieved. She was happy, as were my brother and sisters. I hoped that my mother would live a long and enjoyable life in her new home.

After settling in our new environment, I decided to research colleges for a counseling program. I planned on continuing to work at the Alternative Education Program and attend counseling classes in the evening. I figured it would take at least four years to earn a bachelor's degree.

I found a program at Chicago City and applied for the second semester that started in January. I filled out the necessary forms and asked Floyd and Shelia for recommendations. I received notification that I was accepted in two weeks. I was ecstatic. My letter of acceptance included the possibility of obtaining an academic scholarship for the fall semester. I had achieved my second goal and hoped that my life plan would materialize without a glitch.

My experiences at the alternative program provided the motivation and desire to pursue a counselling degree. I hoped that when I completed the requirements, I could find a position to help disadvantaged youth.

CHAPTER 12
WORK AND SCHOOL

The daily routine at school was thought-provoking. I recognized that helping students with math and occasionally their personal needs was fulfilling but noticed that there was no school spirit. In traditional schools there were social and athletic activities for students.

I gave a lot of thought to approaching Shelia about an activity that both the boys and girls would enjoy. I was active in sports most of my life and knew that team involvement motivated me. I decided to start a basketball team. I came up with several questions I knew Sheila would ask: Would the students be interested? How much would it cost? Who would we play? Where would we play? I could find the answer to the first question by asking some of the kids. I found out that there was some interest, but the enthusiasm did not exist. One of the students was tall, lanky and looked like a ball player. I approached him and told him about my idea. He said, he was interested and would talk to the other boys.

I still had one ace in the hole, Floyd. I remembered that he was a star basketball player at DuShane High School. I stopped by the high school one afternoon and went to his office. He wasn't there. I walked toward the gym and heard a ball swish through a net. There he was. We greeted each other and asked the customary questions...How's it going? How's the family? etc. I discussed my plan with Floyd, and he thought it might work. He asked, "What's your carrot"? I asked, "What do you mean?" He responded, "What's in it for them? What's the payoff?" I understood.

I didn't think about the benefits for the students. I decided to arrange a meeting with a group of students at the end of lunch. I posted information and a date on the hallway bulletin board and hoped that some students would attend. There were approximately two hundred students in the school. A majority were boys. The cafeteria bell rang, and ten students approached the table I was sitting at. I knew two of them including, Josh the athletic-looking student, I had spoken to earlier. I thanked them for coming and explained what I would like to do. Their response was encouraging. Most liked the idea and felt that a basketball team would be fun and would help make the school more like a regular school. They were excited about naming a school mascot and competing with other programs.

The next step was to talk with Sheila. I made an appointment to talk to her at the end of the school day. I knocked on her door and she replied, "Come in." She had just put the phone down and smiled as I entered. "Louis, how can I help you?" she asked. "I don't know if you heard, but I'm interested in starting a basketball team," I said. "I heard, that's a great idea." What are the details?" she asked. I explained everything to her including Floyd's involvement. She said, "I have some extra money in an activity account if you need it." I walked out of Sheila's office walking on air. Now all I had to do was get a team.

I called Floyd to let him know the good news. I told him it was a go. We met the next day to devise a plan. The first question, who would we play? There were a few other alternative programs in Chicago, and we agreed to talk with them. The next question was who would be our team's coach? I looked at Floyd, and he looked at me. It was decided, he would be the coach. Floyd had contacts in the city and knew how to deal with hurdles we would encounter.

To my knowledge there had never been an Alternative Education Program basketball team. Floyd found out that our school would not have to follow the city athletic rules because we were not truly a sanctioned public high school.

Also, there were no rules about a coed team, so our team could include boys and girls. The next step was to contact other schools. That job was mine.

It was the middle of October and basketball season began in November. We were right on target for getting a team together and having our first practice. I posted a tryout notice on the school bulletin board, "Come join our basketball team. Tryouts, Monday, October 12. 4:30 PM, in the gym." Floyd was excited when fourteen students walked through the gym doors. There were ten boys and four girls. Floyd blew his whistle, and we were on our way.

Floyd talked to the students about playing as a team and having fun. The athletes listened intently and asked several questions. "Who are we going to play? Do we have uniforms?" What's our name?" I stepped in and answered their questions. I told them I was trying to find a team to play, we would have shirts, but I don't know our name. One of the girls asked, "How about having a school-wide contest to decide on a name?" "Great idea, would you be interested in arranging the contest?" I asked. Tina said, "I would love to."

There were three other alternative programs in the city, and I contacted them to see if there was an interest. One of the schools, Lincoln Alternative, said they had a team and would play ours. We agreed on Friday, November 3rd at 5:00 PM. We had three weeks to get ready for the game. I finalized all the details with Sheila and Floyd. Sheila gave the team five hundred dollars for shirts and shorts. Floyd coached the team three days a week, selected his starting five, and taught them offensive and defensive plays. Tina had held the "name the team" contest. We were now officially the "AE Cougars."

Game day...the gym was packed with over one hundred excited students. It was new to all. Never had there been a basketball game between two alternative programs. The cougars raced on to the gym floor for their warm up. The fans cheered loudly and chanted, "Go Cougars Go!" The opposing team, AE Hardballs, entered the gym and began their warm up. The Cougar fans watched in silence. The team had three players over six feet tall and looked much more experienced than the Cougars. The ref called the teams to center court. He tossed the ball above two players. The game was on.

The Hardballs pulled ahead easily. The first quarter score was Hardballs 21 and Cougars 10. The students cheered regardless of score. It was the first time they felt like a real school. I watched nervously, hoping that the game would not be marred by a bad call or fight. Floyd kept everything under control making sure that tempers didn't flare, and inappropriate language didn't occur. At half time, we were losing by eighteen points.

Floyd led the team into the locker room and congratulated them on their performance. He encouraged them to work hard and have fun. The team returned to the court and followed his request. The game ended with a Cougar loss, but only in the score. The team and the students had proven that school spirit existed, and fun was possible.

I contacted the other two other alternative programs and gave an update on our game with the Hardballs. Both schools agreed to play the Cougars at our school. Floyd was happy with the outcome of the game and the positivity of the players and student fans. I thanked him for his help. I had talked to the gym teacher about coaching the team for the next two games. He agreed and was anxious to start practice.

I was elated about the outcome. I thanked Sheila, the teachers and students for their help. Our school had achieved a milestone that future alternative programs would follow.

The fall semester ended, and Christmas break was three weeks away. I was walking down the hallway on my way to Mr. S.'s classroom. Tina, whom I had become friends with, asked if our school could have a student dance. I thought the request was great, and told her I would talk to Sheila. She loved the idea. I informed Tina, and she said she would put the details together and share them with me. The dance was titled, "Winter Snowball" and scheduled for January 15th. It was an afternoon dance and nearly fifty students attended. Our school had come one step closer to a traditional high school.

I had followed the curriculum interest of the students during the year and noticed that many of the courses were required by the state and city for graduation. Many students completed the requirements and graduated. Some students just weren't interested in an academic path and were more interested in learning a skill or trade like carpentry, auto mechanics or food services. There were no options available to them in the program. I had heard of schools that offered vocational programs to high school students. I did some research and found a city vocational center close to our school. I talked with Shelia about my idea, and she gave me the okay.

We didn't have a counselor at our school, so I asked a couple of teachers if they were interested in helping me talk to a vocational school about students taking a trade program. Two teachers volunteered, and we met with the nearby vocational school principal. He agreed to four students attending.

We identified two students who met academic and behavior criteria. One chose auto mechanics and the other food services. We arranged for transportation and both started their programs in February. At the end of the school year both students successfully completed their programs and looked forward to the next school year.

The school year ended, and the program had achieved three remarkable outcomes. We had a basketball team, held a school dance and two students were learning a trade. I felt great, the teachers were excited and the students were proud of their newfound "school spirit" and the fun they had.

In addition to the program success, my counseling program at City College was on track. I had completed four courses and was set to take a course during the summer. My efforts at work had solidified my belief in the importance of having a counselor help student with their needs and school morale. I hoped that when my counseling program was completed, a counselor position would be funded.

I worked as a janitor during the summer and completed my counseling course. I started my teacher aide job after Labor Day. I was confident that it would be a great year for the students and me.

I was surprised to learn that Sheila had taken another administrative position and that Mr. S. was the new principal. I greeted him when I passed his office. I said, "Hello and congratulations," he said, "Thank you and please call me Steve." I knew Steve would be a good principal and that he had an interest in creating a counselling position. He asked, "What's the status of your counselling degree?" I told him that I had two years left but needed an internship next year. He said, "Let me know the details and you can meet the requirements here." I said, "Thank you and I'll let you know."

In my second year as a teacher aide, I was assigned to a new teacher. Mrs. George had been teaching math at the school for three years. She was happy to see me, and I was pleased to be her aide. During the year, we played three basketball games, had two dances, and placed three more students in the vocational program. There were a couple of student incidents involving the police which were dealt with by Steve. He understood his role as a principal but desired that a counselor handle teacher, parent, and student issues.

CHAPTER 13

SET BACK

The City College fall semester started, and I took two courses. Both were internship requirements. I noticed that a fellow student was taking the same courses. Her name was Janelle. I approached her after class and learned that she was a part-time student and hoped to become a high school guidance counselor. I told her my background and my plans to counsel at-risk kids. We hit it off immediately and began dating.

Janelle didn't have a car, so I drove her home on Tuesdays and Thursdays. One night, I picked her up in front of the education building and started our customary thirty-minute drive. It was a cold, snowy and icy January evening. As I approached the intersection to her apartment, two frozen in time headlights slammed into the car. The impact was horrific. I was conscious but unable to move my body. I moved my arm toward the passenger's seat, and found that it was empty. The last thing I heard and saw we're screeching sirens and blinking red lights.

I woke up and glanced at my mother who sat by my bedside holding my hand. I looked into her eyes and saw tears flowing down her cheeks. I realized I was in a hospital and noticed machines surrounding my body and wires sticking out of my arms, neck, and head. I couldn't move my body. It was permanently fixed in one position. I tried moving my back, hips, and body. I was as stiff as a board.

I heard the door open and saw a man in a long white coat with a stethoscope around his neck. I didn't have to guess who he was. "How are you feeling?" asked Dr. Peters. I tried to speak but it was difficult. I knew what I wanted to say but the words didn't come out of my mouth. I tried to answer his question. I finally said, "Not good." He walked toward me and sat next to me. My mother squeezed my hand and told me that the doctor would explain everything.

Dr. Peters explained to me that I had been in a car accident and in a coma for two months. I had regained consciousness yesterday. He explained that I had been in critical condition and spent a month in the intensive care unit (ICU). The accident had caused compound fractures in both legs, crushed my pelvis and fractured my backbone. He explained further that I had been placed in a body cast from head to toe but was able to move my arms and hands. He said that I did not seem to have any head trauma and that my brain function wasn't impaired. He went on to say that he would be removing the cast in a couple of weeks to see how much my body had healed. I understood everything that Dr. Peters told me. I had a hundred questions running through my mind but didn't know where to begin asking.

I looked at my mother and asked about Janelle. She sat silently for a few minutes and finally said, "She didn't make it." Tears rolled down my cheeks. "You mean she's dead?" I asked. "Yes, the doctors tried to save her life, but she was thrown out of the car and died on the way to the hospital." I couldn't speak...I was in shock...I wanted to die! The doctor asked the nurse to give me a sedative, and that was the last thing I remembered until the following day.

I woke up alone the next morning. The sun peered through the window blinds, as I opened my eyes. The door opened slowly, and a nurse walked to my bedside. "Good morning and how do you feel?" she asked cheerfully. I looked at her and wanted to tell her exactly how I felt, but I bit my tongue. "Is Dr. Peters here?" I asked. "He makes his rounds around ten, so he should be here then." she responded. I said, "Thank you." The nurse left the room, and I began to think about the questions I had for Dr. Peters.

I dozed off and woke to a gentle knock on the door. I looked up. It was Dr. Peters. He walked toward my bed and stood there waiting for me to ask questions. I started with asking him about Janelle. He told me that he didn't have all the details because she died in the ambulance on the way to the hospital. He said that the impact of the other car caused her to be thrown, and she never regained consciousness. I couldn't believe what he told me. I didn't know what to say.

After several minutes, I asked Dr. Peters to give me the details of my injuries. He told me he would know more after the body cast was removed, but he was confident that my body would heal over time, and I would require months of physical and occupational therapy. I told him I didn't feel any pain. He said I was on morphine and that the amount would gradually be reduced and then eliminated. The pain would start and would be treated with pain medication. I asked him, "Will my injuries heal completely and will I be able to walk?" He said, "I am not sure and everything depends on how well you heal and how hard you work to gain full mobility." He asked if I had any more questions and I said, "No, thank you." I closed my eyes and went to sleep.

I woke up and looked out the window. It was dark...I must have slept the whole day. I looked toward the door as it slowly opened. A nurse walked in carrying a tray of food. I hadn't eaten since early morning, and I was starving. She placed the tray on a bed table and raised the bed to an eating position. I took one look at the tray and assured myself that there was no Chicago hot dog, a slice of pizza or beef sandwich. I had lost my appetite but realized that green beans, mashed potatoes and fish were better than nothing. The nurse left the tray, and I devoured the food in a few minutes. After I ate, I dozed off again and woke up early the next morning

I hadn't had any visitors the prior day. I wondered where my mother was. At ten o'clock the door opened and there stood my mother, brother and two sisters. I was so happy to see them. My eyes began to water. They walked to my bed and gave me a big family hug. I was happy! I told my mother that Dr. Peters said that the body cast would be removed in two weeks, and I would begin therapy. He didn't say what the outcome would be but was pleased with my progress thus far.

My family stayed with me for an hour. We gave a family hug and they left. I thought about two things, the details of the accident and Janelle's death. I had a difficult time accepting her death and the possibility that it was my fault. As for the accident, I wanted to know the exact details and who was responsible? I knew that I wouldn't be able to get out of bed for two weeks and answers to my questions would have to wait.

The two weeks went by slowly. My mother visited every other day. Beside her, I hadn't seen or talked to anyone. I found out that I was not allowed visitors until my body cast was removed.

On the day of the cast removal, Dr. Peters walked into my room as chipper as can be. I wasn't as jovial. I worried that the healing process was not long enough and that my need for morphine to decrease the pain would be addictive. Dr. Peters walked toward my bed accompanied by an attendant holding a saw. Dr. Peters explained the procedure, and I accepted his positiveness. The attendant began sawing the cast from top to bottom. I felt like a baby chick hatching from a shell. The procedure took fifteen minutes. When the doctor finished sawing, I laid there naked as a jaybird.

The cast was set aside, and Dr. Peters began poking me from my neck down. I didn't feel any pain as he prodded. When he finished the examination, he said that he was pleased with the results. My bones and lacerations had healed nicely, and I would be able to use a wheelchair to begin physical therapy. I was happy to hear his comments. I was ready to get out of the bed, resume normal bodily functions and have visitors.

A few hours later two attendants opened the door pushing a wheelchair. I slowly lifted my body from my bed with the help of two attendants. They placed me in the wheelchair, opened the door and whisked me down the hallway. We stopped in front of a door with a sign above that said, "Physical Therapy." I realized this room would be my home for the next couple of weeks prior to my placement in a rehabilitation center. I knew that the cost for my healthcare would be expensive. I was fortunate that my teacher aide job provided health insurance coverage.

The attendants placed me on a table and within a couple of minutes the physical therapist walked into the room. Andrew introduced himself, welcomed me and told me what to expect. The first couple of exercises were painful. He said, "The pain will decrease when your muscles, tendons and cartilage became more pliable."

When the hour of therapy was finished, the same two attendants wheeled me to my room and helped get me back into bed. The routine continued for the next two weeks. During that time, I was allowed visitors. My mother and siblings visited every other day, Floyd came a couple times and Sheila and Steve showed up at night. I was pleased to see them. Steve and I talked about my internship. He said that it was still in the budget and there when I was ready. I hadn't talked to anyone at City College. My coursework was on hold indefinitely.

On my last hospital day, I heard that the kid who rammed into my car had been injured but not seriously. He had been drinking alcohol and was charged with a DUI. His court case was held while I was in the hospital. I was told he was sentenced to jail on a manslaughter charge. His jail term was ten years. I learned later that his name was Jimmy, and he had been a student in the alternative program. I recognized his name immediately and recalled the bathroom smoking incident and his decision to quit school. I decided to visit him in jail when I was healthy.

Two weeks passed, and I was moved to a rehab center to begin the arduous two-month task of using my body again. My legs were as stiff as boards, my midsection was as tight as a drum and my back felt like a steel rod had been placed in the middle of it. All of which was normal for my injuries. I had two hours of physical therapy in the morning and one hour of occupational therapy in the afternoon seven days a week. Within a month, I was able to get in and out of a wheelchair by myself, walk a few steps and move my hips and back. The doctors said my progress was satisfactory and to keep working. Another month passed, and I was evaluated and discharged. I was transported home and my mother and sisters cared for me until I was self-sufficient. The entire recuperation period was six months. I was on target to get back to work and college by September.

CHAPTER 14

BACK ON TRACK

I longed to get back to work and school, but I suddenly realized I didn't have a car. The insurance company had declared it "totaled" and gave me a check for one thousand dollars. Peter and I set out one Saturday morning to search for a car we could share. We walked to neighboring car lots searching for a car that would provide good transportation and reliability. Our first stop was "Gentleman Jake's Car Lot." Jake had a lot of cars on the lot, and I thought we could surely find the right one. We looked at five cars and decided on a 1970 Buick. The price was right. We hoped that we had made the right decision. Peter drove the car off the lot and headed toward our home. He pulled into the driveway and honked the horn. My mother and sisters ran out of the house, hopped in the car, and yelled, "ice cream time."

I felt relieved that I had a car to get back and forth to work and school. Peter and I had arranged a car schedule, so that we would both have access to the car when needed. I had talked to Steve about my return to work. He agreed that I could start at the beginning of the new school year. As customary, I reported to work the day after Labor Day. Mrs. Bea was happy to see me. I settled in quickly and looked forward to a productive year.

I made an appointment with a City College counselor to discuss my return and to review the requirements for graduation. We met just before I started back to work. The counselor's name was Mrs. Collins. She pulled my file from a cabinet and reviewed courses taken and my grade point average (GPA). She said that I had twenty-four credits and my GPA was a 4.0.

I told her about my car accident, and that I hadn't taken any courses since. She was unaware of my accident and encouraged me to return to school and to begin where I left off. I told her I was taking two required internship courses before the accident and would like to register for them. She checked the course schedule and said there was an opening in each. She signed me up on the spot. "By the way," she said, "you are eligible to apply for an academic scholarship next semester. Be certain to apply before November 1st." I thanked her for her help and walked out the door or should I say floated out the door.

I drove home and told everyone about my good news. I was healthy again, had transportation and was returning to work and college. I was "truly back."

The first half of the school year passed quickly. I had applied for the scholarship and would be notified if approved by December 15th. Work was going well. I spent a lot of time helping students with math. A few students approached me with personal concerns, and I made sure that I didn't get too involved. I looked forward to my counseling internship so I could take on a new role and responsibilities.

Interlude Two

I was pleased with the progress I made on my book and anticipated that Latisha would want an update. I enjoyed sharing my life story with her because she frequently offered insights that I had not thought of. I looked up from my laptop and heard a gentle knock. It was Latisha. "How's it going?" Latisha asked. I hadn't given her updates for almost a week. I responded, "Not bad, I have almost one hundred pages and thirty thousand words written." "Wow! sounds like you have been burning the midnight oil," she said. "Would you like to hear what I have written?" I asked. "You bet," she responded.

I began telling Latisha about the Part II chapters. I told her how proud I was to complete the requirements for the two-year associate degree from City

College. I explained to her how the coursework and internship helped me with my success in the alternative program. Latisha spoke, "I know how hard you must have worked to earn the degree and the strength you showed when you had your car accident and Janelle's death. I think that as people read your book they will be inspired with your motivation and determination."

I told Latisha that I had written a chapter on the nurture versus nature issue. She knew that I continually questioned whether my desire to help teens and my resilience were learned or part of my genetic makeup. Latisha knew that my exposure to two distinctly different environments growing up had influenced my personal and political beliefs and opinions. She knew that in my early years, I had lived in a very sheltered environment with little exposure to real life. My high school experience living in the projects and attending DuSable High School contributed to my desire to further my education and make a strong contribution to our community.

Latisha commented, "I believe that your career path decisions, achieving personal goals and balancing work and school were goals that you had set and that nothing would get in the way of achieving them."

In Chapter Four, I had explained that my goals to work with at-risk teens as a counselor and to relocate my mother, brother and sisters to a Hyde Park house were difficult but were achieved. Latisha spoke, "I think that your experience as a teacher aide in the Alternative Education Program gave you the insight for disadvantaged teens. The goal to relocate your family was definitely difficult but you proved not impossible. I know that living in the projects was difficult for your whole family and meeting that goal made you prouder than all your life accomplishments. I am so proud of you, and I think your readers will be too."

When I finished reviewing the chapters, Latisha shared her thoughts and encouraged me to keep writing. I told her I would have an update in a week or so. She got up from her chair and headed toward the kitchen. She turned around abruptly and asked, "Coffee?"

PART III

CHAPTER 15

PRESIDENTIAL ELECTION - 1976

On my first day of college classes, I walked past a table and two students my age asked if I would like to volunteer to work on the presidential election. During the past six months, I had become completely removed from the outside world. I didn't realize it was a presidential election year or who the candidates were? I did recall that Gerald Ford was president. There were several signs posted on walls identifying Jimmy Carter as the Democratic candidate. I had never heard of him, so I did some research. I picked up a couple of brochures and an outline of his platform. I got to thinking that I might get involved in the presidential election.

I finished my two classes and drove home. I pulled the election information out of my school bag and began reading about Jimmy Carter. He was opposing the Republican incumbent candidate Gerald Ford. I began to read about Carter's political background. He was from Georgia and had been the governor. Carter had little national recognition and was a long shot to win the Democratic party nomination, let alone the presidency. His campaign slogan was "A Leader for a Change." In response to the twin nightmares of Vietnam and Watergate, he portrayed himself as an outsider who could clean up the mess in Washington.

I was interested in Carter's national views on health care, social programs, education and civil rights. My opinions and beliefs about the issues were acquired while living in the projects. I witnessed countless children and adults who lived in poverty and struggled with poor health who would benefit from improved social and educational programs. Civil rights continued to be another issue that lacked enforcement.

Carter believed that the federal welfare system for the poor was chaotic and inequitable. It encouraged family instability and did not provide meaningful work incentives. Families were often broken apart because either one parent or the other, usually the mother, needed more income for food, clothing, housing and health care. Many mothers were left to find a job, make the minimum wage and leave their children at home unattended. Many children were forced to live on the streets, make poor decisions and end up involved in a life of crime. Additionally, many poor did not get jobs because the welfare system did not provide support for finding a job, skill training and childcare.

Carter believed that the health care system was also broken and left many poor without routine medical checkups, medication, minor health support and hospitalization for major health diseases, surgeries and rehabilitation. He felt that the current health system needed universal health care, mandatory coverage, national health insurance for all and a better distribution of health care professionals.

Carter emphasized the need for state and local administration of social programs. He felt the federal role should be a constructive one of establishing standards and goals to meet human needs and expend additional resources. He believed that there was a need to provide social service grants to states that provide broad community and family-based support to low-and middle-income households.

He felt that Federal support in education was needed to improve national and state reading and math grade level scores. The student performance of poor children when compared to children from higher family economic status was significantly lower. Other educational areas of concern included improved support for the handicapped, bilingual programs, vocational skill training and early childhood development. School segregation and equitable resources like a broad curriculum, teacher training and building maintenance were still left unresolved. More federal support was needed for states and local school districts.

Carter thought that despite the efforts of the Civil Rights Act of 1964 that emphasized the equal treatment of all regardless of race, color, sex, religion, age, language, national origin, discrimination, bias, and prejudice still existed in states, cities and local communities across America. He emphasized that many poor did not participate fully in economic, social and political processes. Fair housing enforcement, race and economic integration, school choice and higher education support continued to be neglected at state and local levels. [26]

After reading Carter's views on health care, social service programs, education and civil rights, I concluded that his opinion about each issue was in line with my beliefs. I needed to read more, research each issue more thoroughly before fully committing to volunteering to work on his campaign. I continued reading and talking to several other students. I decided to join the Young Democratic Association (YDA) with the challenge to win the 1976 presidential election.

I realized that Carter's political platform was extremely broad and encompassing. I supported many of his views on national issues that he was concerned with and wanted to change. I believed that there should be less federal control and more state and local involvement in health, social, education and civil rights legislation, particularly decision-making and funding.

My more immediate interest and concern were education and social service needs of disadvantaged families and children. I was a strong proponent of integrated schools, equalizing school resources (i.e., curricula, support services, teacher preparation/certification, and building maintenance). A focus on these educational issues demanded that states and communities make decisions based on specific local needs.

I decided I would get involved in the Carter presidential campaign by making phone calls, distributing information door-to-door and participating in rallies. The broader issues of his campaign were left for others. My concern and interest in education and social service improvements would become my passion and career commitment.

Carter won the 1976 election and served one term. His platform and ideology had succumbed to the economic pressure. Americans believed in his universal causes, but the impact of high costs for food, housing, gas, and personal needs hit home.

Despite being a single term president, I was pleased with my participation. I had successfully had a hand in electing a US president. After he won, I celebrated with my fellow workers and looked forward to his policy impact on the poor. I observed Carter's presidency for four years and watched his efforts to achieve his platform goals. The economic factor loomed over his plans to achieve his goals and he left after four years on a negative note.

My direct involvement in politics ended with Carter and Reagan. I concluded that if I were going to help poor white and black youth, it would be "hands on." I planned to continue to work at the alternative school, support students as an internship counselor, complete my bachelor's degree and find a counselor position in the South Side community.

In 1980, Carter was defeated in a landslide by Republican Ronald Reagan. His platform emphasized across-the-board tax cuts to stimulate the economy. Reagan's policies resulted in less money being spent in education and social programs. His presidency was regarded as successful in respect to a decrease in inflation and unemployment, national pride, foreign policy, and tax reform. Reagan followed a "trickle down" economic theory which held that taxes on businesses and the wealthy should be reduced to offer more support to the middle-class and poor. I felt that xhis theory was counter-productive, and that federal money should be appropriated with criteria and structure to states and cities to meet local education and social needs. [27]

CHAPTER 16

INTERNSHIP

The first semester of college was nearly over, and I had earned six more credits toward my bachelor's degree. More importantly, I had completed the two courses required for an internship. When I got home from school my mother handed me my mail. On the top of three letters was an envelope from City College. I had been waiting for the results of my scholarship application. I opened the letter nervously, hoping it was good news. I read, "Dear Mr. Van Patton, City College is pleased to inform you that a partial scholarship has been awarded to you for the spring semester." I literally jumped for joy! My mother heard my jubilation and ran into the living room. I told her the good news, and she gave me a big hug.

The following day I knocked on Steve's door and told him about the scholarship, and that I had completed the coursework for the counselor internship. He said, "Great! Let's get you started next week." I informed Mrs. Bea about my internship, and she congratulated me. "Hope I can find a replacement by next week who can help the students with math," she responded.

Steve had found a small office for me next to the gym. I realized that it would be noisy, but it didn't matter. I was finally going to have direct contact with kids and families that need support.

Monday morning came quickly. I was set up in my tiny office with no windows and listening to the constant pounding of a basketball on the gym floor. I waited patiently for my first student. After two hours, I realized that no one was coming. Steve had told me that he would talk to the teachers to get referrals. I went to his office and asked if any teachers had approached him about students requesting counseling support. He said he had talked with the teachers, and that he had asked them to refer students to me. I immediately realized that teachers would not voluntarily refer students nor would students automatically knock on my door. One of the basic principles of counseling was to build trust with teachers and students.

I decided that different strategies were needed. I started visiting classrooms, eating in the cafeteria and hanging out in front of school in the morning and afternoon. Within a few days, several students started talking to me and asked about my job. I explained that I was a counselor and available if they needed help with personal, school, or family issues. I attended faculty meetings and explained my role, several questions were asked including confidentiality. I told the teachers that referrals and their information would be held in strict confidence.

The next day, I noticed a student walking by my office. The door was wide open, and he looked in but kept walking toward the gym. I sat behind my desk and continued reading. A few minutes passed, and I got up to see if the student was still there. He stood next to the gym and looked nervously at me. He asked, "Are you the counselor?" "Yes, I said. "My name is Louis." He asked to talk to me. I said, "Sure, come into my office." His name was Mike. "How can I help you?" He explained that he was being bullied by a student in his class and wanted to know what to do about it. I gave him a couple of suggestions and told him to let me know if they worked. A couple of days passed, and I saw Mike standing in the hallway with a kid twice his size. They seemed to get along. I wondered if the boy was the one who bullied him. I saw Mike leaving school at the end of the day. I approached him and asked, "Was the boy you were talking to earlier the bully?" He said, "Yes," It looked like you were getting along, how did that happen?" I asked. "He is in my math class, and I noticed he struggled with math. I took your advice and offered to help him," Mike responded. "Great!" I said. "Thanks for your help," he said. Mike walked away and met up with his new friend.

I started getting a couple of referrals from teachers each week. Most students struggled with their schoolwork. They had a desire to do well but needed reading and math tutoring. I talked to Steve about an early morning or after-school program where students could get extra reading and math help, academic support and homework assistance. He said he would ask a few teachers if they were available to provide support. Two teachers said "yes" and the academic support program was underway.

Several students approached me about drug, relationship, peer, and family issues during the six-month internship. I tried to provide as much advice as possible. I was helpful with some students and not with others. I realized that achieving total success was impossible, but if I were able to help some students, I was pleased.

The last half of the school year and my internship ended in June. Steve was pleased with my work and wanted to budget a counselor position for the next school year. I had one remaining year left in the counseling program, and I would earn my degree. I was excited about the possibility of a full-time job with the alternative program. My summer janitorial job had started, and I began to think about what I would do in September. My counselling internship was finished, and I had hoped that Steve would offer a full-time position. When I got home from work, I opened the door and heard the phone ringing. I answered the phone, "Hi Louis, this is Steve, are you interested in working full time as a counselor in September?" I immediately said, "Yes." "Can you meet tomorrow to talk about it?" "Sure," I responded, what time?" "How about ten o'clock in my office.?" he answered. "I'll be there," I replied. We met the next day and Steve explained that the job was temporary because I had not finished the counseling program and my bachelor's degree. He said, "City College had agreed to supervise the position and the school district will pay your salary." I was thrilled and could hardly wait until September. I picked up my mop and pushed my pail down the hallway to the cafeteria.

CHAPTER 17

PART OF THE JOB

The new school year started as usual the day after Labor Day. I stood outside the front door and watched the students shuffle into the school. I recognized a few of them from my work as a teacher aide and as an intern counselor. A couple of kids said "hi" to me, and I returned the greeting. I walked toward my new office located next to the library. I was going to miss balls bouncing on the gym floor and the basketball backboard. Steve had a nameplate placed on my door. I felt like a real professional counselor and ready to provide support to teachers, students and families.

My work began with a knock on the door. In walked one of the teachers. "Hello," I said to Mrs. Brown." "How can I help you?" I asked. She said, "One of my students came to class with bruises on her face, and I asked what happened? The student said nothing, began to cry and laid her head on the desk. When the bell rang to end the period, she vanished into the crowded hallway." "What's her name?" I inquired. Mrs. Brown said, "Marcy." "Okay, I will look into it," I said. Mrs. Brown left, and I went to the guidance office to look up Marcy's class schedule. It was the fourth period, and she was assigned to a cafeteria study hall. I walked to the cafeteria and asked the study hall teacher to point Marcy out to me. She was not in her assigned seat. I went back to the guidance office to look up her home address and phone number. I called the number and no one answered. I knocked on Steve's door and told him about the issue. He was concerned and told me to keep calling and let him know if Marcy comes to school the next day. I waited patiently outside the front door the next day hoping to see a girl with bruises on her face. I watched each student enter school but did not see a girl with bruises. I went back to my office and called the telephone number I called the previous day. The phone rang six times and a girl answered. "Hello," she spoke. "Is this Marcy," I asked. She responded tentatively in a low-pitched voice. "Yes, "she said. "Hi, this is Louis, a counselor at your school. I was looking for you yesterday and wanted to talk to you." "Why," she asked? I decided to be honest and told her that Mrs. Brown was concerned about some bruises on her face. She told me that she had fallen and that's how she got the bruises. I questioned her response and asked if she would be in school tomorrow. She said, "Yes."

I told Mrs. Brown that I had spoken to Marcy about the bruises. I told her that Marcy said she fell and that was the reason for the injury. We both questioned her answer because she had started to cry and put her head on her desk when Mrs. Brown asked her what happened to her face. I asked Mrs. Brown to send Marcy to my office when she came to her class. I wasn't sure that Marcy would come to school or to my office. I waited anxiously for a knock on my door. The knock didn't come but the handle on the door turned slowly and opened slightly. I looked up from my desk and saw a short, dark haired young lady looking at me. I said, "Hi, is your name Marcy?" She said, "Yes." "Please come in and take a seat." I spoke. Marcy sat down and sheepishly looked out the window. I told her that Mrs. Brown and I were concerned about the bruises on her face.

She reiterated her excuse that she had fallen. She suddenly broke into a sob and trembled uncontrollably. I talked calmly to her and fortunately she stopped crying. I asked if she wanted to talk, and she nodded. She said that her father had a bad temper when he drank and that he had hit her when she tried to talk to him. I asked her about her mother and siblings. She said her mother had left two years ago. and she had no brothers or sisters. I told her that it was my responsibility to report the incident to social services and that there was a possibility she would be separated from her father. She said that her father had hit her several times. She said that she was afraid of her father and didn't want to live with her father any longer.

I called social services and told them about Marcy. They said a counselor would come to school and talk to Marcy at two o'clock. I waited with Marcy for two hours until the counselor came. Marcy explained everything to the counselor and left with her. Before she entered the hallway, she turned and looked at me and said, "Thank you." I felt like I had helped her and hoped her future would be better.

I continued receiving referrals from teachers, and a few students dropped by my office to tell me their problems. With each case, I provided as much support as possible. I was successful with some and not with others. I realized how fortunate I was to have my job.

I arrived at school early on the Monday after Thanksgiving break. I sat quietly in my office and waited for my eight o'clock appointment. Suddenly, I heard a loud bang coming from the hallway. I knew that sound and heard it often when I lived in the projects. It was the sound of a single shot from a gun. I got up from my chair and ran into the hallway. I saw a boy lying on the ground and another holding a pistol standing next to him. The boy looked up at me and pointed the gun at my head. I put my hands in the air and said, "Put the gun down!" He continued to point it at me. I moved closer to him, and he did not move. I moved closer and closer until I was almost touching the gun. The boy rocked back and forth, and the gun swayed with him. I realized that he was scared and the only chance I had to stop him and save my life was to grab the gun. I did it. As I grabbed the gun from him a shot rang out. I held the gun in my hand and clutched my shoulder. I was hit. Several teachers reached the boy and pulled him to the floor. The police had been called and ran to aid the teachers. The police cuffed him and walked him away from the scene.

Holding my shoulder, I bent down to check on the boy lying on the hallway floor. The EMTs had already tried to revive him, but they were too late. He was dead! I tried to stand up, but my legs gave way beneath me. I woke up in the hospital. My mother, brother and sisters sat near my bedside. I felt a little groggy but otherwise was in no pain. My shoulder was in a sling.

A doctor knocked on the door and walked toward the bed. "How are you feeling?" he asked. I said, 'Not too bad after taking a bullet." He and my family laughed. He said I was lucky, and that the bullet had passed through my shoulder and there was no structural, muscle, or tendon damage. He said that I could go home. He gave me some pain medication and turned to leave the room. He turned around and looked at me and said, "It was a pleasure treating a hero."

I returned to school in two days and was greeted at the door by a large group of teachers and students. Many of them patted me on the back and thanked me for my heroism. I thanked them back, but humbly felt that I was just doing my job.

The boy who had shot me and killed the other boy was charged with first degree murder and sentenced to a twenty-year jail term. The shooting was about a drug deal gone wrong. I read about the incident in the newspaper. A third page paragraph in the Chicago Tribune read, "Counselor Shot at School." After reading the article, I finally realized that I could have been killed. I had never given any thought to a school being unsafe let alone where a murder would take place. I wondered what the future would bring.

CHAPTER 18

JOB OFFER

The school year ended in June and so did my internship. I had completed my coursework and internship successfully and looked forward to graduation and my bachelor's degree. I went to the ceremony by myself. I didn't want to make a big deal out of it. The shooting incident and the support I had given to teachers, students and families during the school year had strengthened my resolve and commitment to working in the social services field.

Before applying for a counselor's position, I needed to learn more about what was available in the Chicago area. I researched the Chicago Child Care Society to learn about their services. I found that it was the oldest child welfare organization in Illinois (125 years 1849-1974). I was looking for information about their counseling program. I had picked up a pamphlet at City College that provided a description and offered a list of programs and services. [28]

First on the list was counseling. The program provided family-oriented counseling for the agency's foster care programs and the Child and Family Development Center. Additionally, individual and family therapy, clinical consultation and training were offered to the community. I continued reading the pamphlet and learned about the educational support program, extended family option, traditional foster care, and teen services. I was overwhelmed with the amount of information and number of programs CCCS offered to the community. I called the Center office and asked to speak to personnel. I was transferred to an administrator, and I asked what the procedure was to apply for a counselor position. She explained the application process and informed me that there were two vacancies, and she would send an application to me in the mail.

I received the application within two days and filled it out immediately. I decided to submit the application in person. It would give me an opportunity to identify the location and how long it would take to get there for my interview. I walked up the steps and pushed open the huge metal doors. It felt like I was walking into a bank vault. A receptionist greeted me as I walked toward a visitor's seating section. I told the receptionist that I wanted to apply for a counselor position. I started to hand the application to the receptionist when a woman in a business suit approached her desk. The receptionist said "Hi." to the woman. She said, "June, this young man is applying for a counselor position and was just giving his paperwork to me. "Thanks Meg, I will take it." June was the Director of Counseling Services. June looked at me and asked, "Didn't I talk to you on the phone the other day?" "Yes," I spoke. "Would you like to come up to my office and tell me about yourself?" she asked. "I certainly would," I said. We took the elevator to the third floor. She asked me to sit down while she reviewed my application, resume and references.

When she finished reading, she looked up at me. "Very impressive," she said. "Your experience with the alternative program was unique. We don't have many applicants with your background. I read that you served two internships: one at the beginning of your studies and another to complete the requirements for your bachelor's degree. Please tell me about some of your experiences with students, families and teachers," she asked. I told her about my contact with students, and the support and advice I gave to them about family, drug, academic and bullying issues. I mentioned my "start-ups" at the school...basketball team, tutoring program and social events. She sat back in her chair and suddenly rocked forward. "What about the shooting at your school?" she asked. I was surprised she brought that incident up because I had not mentioned it on my application or resume. "Well." I spoke. "I didn't want to mention the shooting because it detracts from other things that I have accomplished." "Quite humble," she remarked. She said that she was considering offering me a counselor position but would like to schedule a formal interview with her team and check my references. She said that she would call and schedule the interview. I thanked for her time and told her that I looked forward to hearing from her.

I walked out of June's office and gave myself a slap on the cheek. Was I dreaming or did I just have an interview for a counselor position? The phone rang three days later, and I jumped from my chair to answer it. "Hello," said June. "Are you still interested in the counselor position?" she asked. I said, "I am." June asked if I could interview with her team on Friday at ten o'clock?" I said, "Yes." I was excited about the interview and could hardly control my emotions during the rest of the week. I woke up early Friday morning anxious about the interview. I arrived at the Center fifteen minutes early and waited to be called. I looked up and saw June. "Are you ready?" She asked. I got up from my seat and followed her into a conference room. There were four people in the room. Each person gave their name and position. The interview lasted an hour. Each person took turns asking questions like: "What are my future goals?" "How long did I plan on being a counselor?" "What family poverty experiences did I have?" I did my best to answer the questions as thoughtfully and as succinctly as possible. June spoke for the group and said she would get back to me on Monday.

Monday arrived, I got home at five o'clock and heard the phone ring as I opened the door. I answered the phone and said, "Hello." June responded, "Would you like a job with CCCS?" "Yes, I would," I spoke. "Great! Can you fill the paperwork out on Wednesday and start on Monday?" she asked. "Yes, I can." I spoke. The phone clicked off, but I stood holding it to my ear. "I have a job," I screamed.

I informed my family of the good news, called Floyd, Steve and Sheila and told them about my new job. They congratulated me and expressed how happy they were for me. I had been working toward this goal for ten years, and I finally achieved it. It was a tough road at times...the student overdose and death, my car accident, Maria's death, Jimmy's jail sentence, and the school shooting. All the incidents were traumatic and would follow me for life and hopefully help me be a good counselor.

CHAPTER 19

FAMILY UPDATE

My school and work progress had gone well. Our family continued to live in the small house in Hyde Park. It was crowded at times, but I enjoyed being with my family. I had thought about getting my own place but couldn't afford it. I hoped that the salary from my new job would motivate me to move to my own apartment.

My mother still worked at the meat packing plant. She had finished her twenty-fifth year. She was approaching fifty-five and was near retirement. She hoped to work another five years. She remained healthy and was able to manage work, house responsibilities and spend time with her friends. I recognized that she had worked hard her entire life and retirement would be a dream come true.

My brother, Peter, had turned twenty-eight and worked as a manager at Radio Shack. He had moved out of the family home and was planning to get married in a few months. He had bought a new car, and I had inherited the car we had bought together a few years ago. It was on its last leg and needed to be replaced.

My sister, Rosie, had completed college and was teaching English at Hyde Park High School. She was fortunate to have her college paid for through a federal teacher's training program. She was married and lived in an apartment close to the school. She enjoyed working with teens and hoped to work at Hyde Park for several years.

Mindy, the baby of the family, was a nurse. She received her RN through a mental health training program and her bachelor's degree from City College. She lived with my mother and helped my mother when needed.

We had all become successful and worked in fields that offered support and help to our community. I often thought that the two years we spent living in the projects and going to segregated schools influenced our decision to choose work that would be supportive and rewarding.

CHAPTER 20

REPORTING FOR DUTY

I woke up bright and early for the first day of my new job. I entered the front door and was greeted by Meg, the receptionist whom I had met earlier. "Good morning and welcome to CCCS," she spoke. I said good morning to her and walked toward the elevator. Meg asked, "Do you know where your office is located?" I said, "No." "Third floor, room 319", she said. I said, "Thanks." When I got to the third floor, I looked for room 319. It was located at the end of the hall next to the janitor's supply room. My mind flashed back to my work with Floyd and at the alternative program. I hoped that I didn't have to work a dual role again. I opened the door and was greeted by June and her team. They all welcomed me and gave me a few gifts...a pen, notebook, and a rolodex. I put two and two together and knew exactly what the gifts were for. "Meeting at ten in the team room." June yelled.

At ten o'clock, I walked to the team room and sat with the other counselors. There were five of us. In walked June and she said, "Let's get started with our assignments."

June asked each of us which family services programs we were interested in working. I said, "I would like to concentrate on the counseling, educational and foster care programs." She acknowledged that my choices were well chosen based on my experiences.

June explained that the counseling program provides family-oriented counseling for the agency's foster care and child and family development center.

Individual and family therapy is provided to the clients. The services include individual case consultation and training.

She described that the educational support program provides services to children who are experiencing academic, behavioral and attendance difficulties and are at risk of future expulsion or dropping out of school. CCCS works with local community schools and other service providers with the aim of providing children with a more stable school experience.

She described that the traditional foster care program works with children who have been removed from the care of their parents due to issues of abuse, neglect, or abandonment. The program places children in a CCCS licensed foster home or in a home of another family member. The program works toward adoption or guardianship.

When June finished providing information about each program, I asked her about the starting procedure. She said, "I will assign you two cases in each of the three programs." She gave me six folders, and I walked to my office and read the details of each. I decided that my reports would include a description of the case, identification of support strategies and an explanation of the resolution.

Case one was labeled *Counseling*. The case information identified a family in need for individual counseling for a six-year-old child. For confidential reasons, I decided to name the family or individuals involved with a pseudonym. I named this case, "Jupiter."

The family had not been assigned a counselor previously and this was their first request for support. The parents expressed they were having difficulty controlling their son's behavior. He was acting out in school, home, and other settings. He would not listen to their requests to behave and frequently would intensify his behavior when told to calm down. I realized that his behavior could be caused by several reasons. My first step was to call the parents, introduce myself and ask them to meet with me. I arranged a meeting and met the following day without their son. They reiterated their concern and listened to my questions. They revealed that their son had lost his dog to a car accident and has acted inappropriately since the incident. Despite their attempts to console him, his behavior did not improve. Of course they told their son that they would get another dog, but that did not help. I explained that their son may be going through a grieving process and may benefit from grief counseling. I told them that grieving over the loss of a pet, particularly for a child, is like grieving over the death of a relative or friend.

I suggested they talk about their son's dog often and with love. I recommended they let their son know that while the pain will go away; the happy memories of the dog will always remain. They were pleased with the recommendations and thanked me. I told them to let me know the outcome and, if needed, I would provide counseling to their son. I felt pleased that I had provided the support and hoped it would work.

Case two was labeled *Counseling*. The case information indicated the husband and wife were having marriage problems. I labeled it as "Mars." The case type was new to me. I hadn't been exposed to marriage issues during my internships or life experiences. I read the file carefully trying to pinpoint the difficulties the couple were having. The information suggested that it was work-related. He was a salesman and frequently went on business trips. She was stuck at home with two young children. She was an accomplished artist and had shown her work in respected local galleries. Their obvious problem was that he was on the road, and she was unable to use her creative painting skills. They were on the verge of a divorce but wanted to see a counselor before making that decision. I decided to call them and invite them to my office.

The couple met with me, and they expressed their love for each other but could not compromise on a solution. He realized that he should spend more time at home, and she expressed her desire to paint and be more active in the art world. I asked a few questions but primarily allowed them to discuss their issues with each other. As the session progressed, they began to come up with their own conclusions.

The outcome was their decision. They decided that he would not travel on the weekends, and she would use one of the days to paint. They were pleased with their decision and asked if I would be available for future sessions. I said I would and scheduled them for three weekly sessions. After they left, I sat back in my chair and breathed a sigh of relief. I thought, I had helped the couple agree to a solution and to future counselling sessions.

Case three was labeled *Education*. I was extremely comfortable providing support for children experiencing academic, behavioral and attendance issues and at risk of future expulsion or dropping out of school. My two internships in the alternative program had provided the experience needed to provide school support. I read the file and learned that the parents were concerned with their daughter's desire to drop out of school. I named the file "Venus." She was fifteen and had fallen two grade levels behind her peers. She was in ninth grade and her friends were in the eleventh grade. I couldn't identify the reasons why she was two years behind. I decided to call her parents to get more information. They agreed to talk with me. I scheduled the meeting within a week. The parents and their daughter knocked on my door. I invited them in and greeted them with the customary comments."How are you? Thanks for coming."

The girl's name was Helena. She was short, heavyset and extremely nervous. She stared out the window and showed extraordinarily little eye contact. I asked her parents a few questions about her academic progress. They told me that her reading skills had always been low and that her inability to comprehend information affected her grades in other subject areas. I looked at Helena and asked if she would like to contribute to our conversation. She looked at me shyly and agreed.

I asked her when she first noticed that she had reading difficulties. She responded, "I think in fifth grade, but I was able to keep up learning by seeing." I asked, "What does that mean?" She said that she would visualize in her head the answers to a written question but as the information got harder it was difficult to keep up." Based on my educational experience, I suspected that Helena had a learning problem and required special support. I also suspected that she needed therapy. My knowledge was limited with both needs, so I recommended that Helena and her parents consult a psychologist. It was a difficult decision, because I was not confident about her needs, but a referral for therapy might help. Helena's parents seem reluctant regarding my recommendation an indicated they would think about it and left. I sat back in my chair and said to myself, "I did my best."

Case four was labeled *Education.* The next referral was from a local elementary school. A teacher requested a counselor assignment to the school to talk to the kindergarten class about peer influence. I identified the case as "Pluto." I called the teacher, Mrs. Jones, and told her I had read the request and would like to visit with her to get more information. I met with her after school on the following Tuesday. She told me that a student in the class had been stealing candy from a small delicatessen located near the school. The boy who stole the candy shared it with the others and they would not name the kid involved. The teacher had a conference with all the parents without success. The kids told their parents they were not "rats."

I said that I would meet with the class the next day. I arrived at nine o'clock and the kids were assembled in the gym. Mrs. Jones sat with us. I looked at the group and was convinced they weren't all angels. My goal was to identify the kids who were stealing. I thought if I could do that there would be no "ratting" and I could talk with them separately. I noticed one boy with a large bulge in his front pant pocket. I asked his name and he said, "Paul." I asked him what he had in his pants pocket, and he said, "candy." I asked if I could have some and he responded, "Sure." I took the candy and asked where it came from. He said, "The candy store on the corner." I thanked him for sharing. He said, "I have been sharing with all the kids." I asked him if he thought that as long he shared that it was okay to steal the candy. He said, "My parents told me sharing was okay and that's why I stole and gave candy to my friends." From a five-year-old's perspective, he didn't think that it was wrong. I told Paul that I would like to talk about stealing and sharing with him. He said, "Okay." I reached out to his parents, and we discussed the issue. They agreed to talk with Paul and explain that stealing to share is not okay. I walked away from the school chuckling. I thought Paul's parents better keep an eye on him as gets older. I child's mind is not fixed and providing early support often helps change misguided actions.

Case five was labeled *Foster Care.* I read the details of the case and learned that a mother was appealing the social service's department decision to remove her four children from her care because of abuse. I identified the case as "Uranus." Additional information suggested that the abuse occurred while her former boyfriend lived with her. He had moved from her home, and she no longer allowed him to have contact with her children. She argued that the social service department had no knowledge of the current circumstances. The report named the case worker assigned to the case as Latisha Browne. I called her to ask for a meeting. The receptionist said she was in the field and wouldn't return to the office until six o'clock. I worked until five but decided to extend the day and call her. I called her at six-fifteen and she answered the phone after seven rings. "Hello, she said. "This is Latisha, how can I help you?" she asked. I told her my name was Louis, and I worked for CCCS. I informed her that I was assigned a foster care case that involved the removal of a woman's four children because of abuse. I explained the details and the mother's comments about her boyfriend. Latisha was familiar with the case but not the details of the updated situation. She said she would follow up on the case and would let me know the outcome.

Three days later the phone rang. "Hello," Louis spoke. "This is Latisha from Social Services. How are you?" she asked. I said," I am well and am happy that you've called." She advised me that she had followed up on the foster care case and would monitor the situation. She said, "The children will not be removed from the home if the boyfriend does not return and abuse the children." I thanked Latisha for her help and asked if I could stay in contact with her. She said that would be fine. We ended our conversation with "Hope to talk to you soon."

Case six was labeled *Foster Care.* The case detailed the need for a foster care placement in a family member's home. I identified the case as "Earth." There was a problem with the placement because the placement family could not manage all five children. They were willing to take three of the children. CCCS has a rule to place children from the same family with each other. There were times when that is difficult to do. I decided that I needed help. I called Latisha and explained the situation. She was familiar with situations like this, and said she would contact the foster family and find a placement for the other two children.

Latisha called me in a week and said that she hadn't found a placement. She said she would work on the case and that may take a while. I thanked her for her help. I realized that foster care was a huge issue and that placements were often difficult to find. I knew Latisha would do her best.

I scheduled an appointment to meet with June to update her on the six cases. We met in her office the following day. I described the procedures used, beginning with identifying each case with a pseudonym. She said, "Quite creative." I explained that I read each case thoroughly, contacted a source, came up with solutions and resolved each as well as possible. She asked several questions and congratulated me on my first assignment. She looked down at her desk and picked up a handful of folders. She said, "Here's your new caseload." I returned to my office and placed the folders on my desk. I counted thirty-one cases. I thought to myself. This was going to be a busy month.

CHAPTER 21
JIMMY

Four years had passed since my car accident, and I had fully recovered from my broken legs, crushed pelvis and broken back. The doctors were shocked that I recovered so well. I recalled the rehabilitation therapy that I did for six months. It was extremely painful and exhausting. At times, I wanted to give up but kept working. The encouragement my family and friends gave me was relentless, and I thanked them frequently.

I thought about my friend Janelle whenever I heard an ambulance or saw a car accident. She was just twenty-two when she was killed in the car accident. We would often talk about the work we would like to accomplish when we graduated from college. I am certain we would have worked together to achieve our career goals.

Jimmy, the teenager who was driving the car that hit us was driving drunk, charged with manslaughter and sentenced to a ten-year prison term. I had met a couple of correction officers, and they gave me information about Jimmy. He had served four years of his sentence and was eligible for parole in two years.

I found out that Jimmy was serving his sentence in a medium-security prison located in Pekin, Illinois. It was a federal medium-security correctional institution for male inmates. It was one hundred seventy-five miles from Chicago.

I had promised myself that I would visit Jimmy when I was released from the hospital. I had met Jimmy as a court-placed student in the alternative program. I caught him smoking in the men's room and reported him to Sheila, the principal. He was assigned to the alternative program as a last chance option and would be placed in a juvenile detention center if he broke a school rule.

I was disappointed when I heard Jimmy had quit school and hoped he would turn his life around. Instead, he continued to get involved in unlawful acts. The reports that I had obtained provided a lengthy description of all his encounters with breaking the law. He was caught robbing a store and spent a year in a juvenile detention center. He spent six months in the city jail on a drunk and disorderly charge. His unlawful actions led to his losing his driver's license. The night of the accident he had stolen a car, gotten drunk and was driving twenty miles an hour above the speed limit.

The accident was hard to forget. I felt a need to visit him in jail. I made all the necessary contacts to schedule an appointment to talk to him. On the day of the visit, I made the three-hour drive to the Pekin medium-security prison. I wasn't sure what we would talk about but thought the visit would offer closure to a tragedy that still bothered me. When I arrived at the prison, I was escorted to a small room with a table and chair separated by a plexiglass barrier. A black old-fashioned phone hung on the wall next to the table. I was extremely nervous while I waited for Jimmy to sit on the other side of the glass. Fifteen minutes passed, and he shuffled into the room with his head looking at the floor. He knew I was coming and had agreed to the visit.

Jimmy sat down and picked up his phone. I picked mine up also. At first, neither of said a word. Finally, I said, "Thank you for seeing me." He said nothing. I continued trying to have a conversation with him. At one point he picked his head up and looked me straight in the eyes and said, "I am sorry." I felt some relief because his apology was exactly why I wanted to meet with him. I wanted him to show remorse for killing Janelle and causing my injuries. He placed the phone back on the hook, stood up and walked out the door. That was the last time I saw him or heard anything about him. Based on his unlawful history, I suspected he would continue a life of crime and spend more years in prison.

On my drive back to Chicago, I felt pleased with my visit. I thought about Jimmy's encounters with the law and the influence his peers, family or environment affected his poor choices. I concluded that one of the best options to help at-risk kids was to offer support in their early years. When I got back to work the next day, I talked to June about an early intervention program to reduce generational involvement in unlawful acts. She suggested that I submit a proposal and she would see if it had merit.

CHAPTER 22

DIFFERENT PROPOSAL

"I now pronounce you husband and wife!" The words echoed through the courthouse's tall rafters, beams, and ceilings.

Latisha and I had been dating for two years and continually talked about getting married. I decided that the timing was right, so I mustered up the nerve to propose. I made the decision one spring evening as we jogged along a path on our way to our small apartment near Hyde Park. When we reached the locked apartment door, I opened it with trepidation. As Latisha stepped back to enter, I looked at her and asked, "Will you marry me?" She said, "Now or after I shower." I laughed and said to myself, "Why did I ask her to marry me at such an unromantic moment?" "I mean not this exact minute but in the future." I said, Latisha responded, "You mean a year or two from now?" "No, how about we apply for a marriage license and decide then." I spoke. "Louis, you realize that it takes months to plan a wedding," she responded. We had never talked about the details of a wedding...where? guests, ceremony, etc. "How about we get cleaned up and go to a restaurant to talk about the details," I suggested. She agreed.

I had met Latisha's mother and father a few times but didn't really know them well. I knew that they had moved from Mississippi to Chicago thirty years ago when Latisha was five years old. They moved from a small town where her father worked as a laborer on a farm. His wife, Brionna, worked alongside him every day picking vegetables in the summer and harvesting tobacco in the fall. Life in a southern state was difficult for blacks. Most of the farm work was hot, dirty, and backbreaking. Racial discrimination was rampant and not addressed by politicians or law enforcement. The promise of a better life in Chicago was alluring. Latisha's uncle got her father a steel plant job. The opportunity to leave the sharecropping fields to make more money and have a better life for Latisha were their motivators.

Latisha's parents settled into a small apartment on the south side of Chicago and began a new city life far from the rural lifestyle they were used to. Latisha often commented that the change was difficult but they persevered...her parents wanted a better life for her than they had.

Latisha's father was a hard worker and made a good impression at the steel plant. He learned specific jobs easily and volunteered for overtime when asked. Her mother worked at a dry-cleaning store washing and ironing clothes. Latisha was school age when she moved to Chicago and was enrolled in kindergarten at a neighborhood public school. She was a good student and was always concerned with the welfare of her peers. More than once, she came to the aid of a classmate being bullied or crying because of family problems. It didn't take long for Latisha to realize her life work would be helping children.

Latisha completed grade school, junior high and high school with honors. Her sensitivity and empathy prompted her to and enroll in the social work program at the University of Chicago. She excelled at the university and began working at the Chicago Social Services Organization (CSSO) upon graduation. She worked at CSSO when we met and graciously agreed to help with my research at CCCS.

Latisha loved children and families and would often get too involved in her cases. She had difficulty separating her work life from her personal life. She recognized the problem and received weekly therapy. The therapist helped her compartmentalize her social work responsibilities and stressed the importance of balancing them with her personal life. Our relationship developed into a friendship and companionship that we both needed.

We sat down at a cozy and private table at one of our favorite restaurants. We were both eager to continue our conversation about marriage and delayed our food order. I ordered a beer and Latisha had a glass of wine. We began discussing our options about getting married. We agreed that we didn't want a church ceremony, large reception, or a lot of guests. Our decision was to get married in the courthouse by a judge and have a small party at her parents' apartment. The marriage was set for Friday the thirteenth, May 1, 1984. With everything set, we ordered our food and enjoyed the rest of the evening.

Only one thing missing, a ring. I found a local neighborhood jeweler and Latisha and I went to pick out our wedding rings. They were simply designed and frail looking but strong enough to last through a lifelong marriage.

Our wedding party included Latisha's parents, my family, and our friends. All enjoyed the party. It wasn't much of a celebration...music played softly in the living room, the home-cooked food was laid out, bottles of champagne were uncorked, and cake was served. The party lasted a few hours. We thanked everyone, said goodbye, and drove to our apartment. We were an incredibly happy couple starting a life together with the promise of a long life. On Monday, we returned to work to do what we loved the most...help families and children.

CHAPTER 23
LATISHA

I returned to my work and was greeted by our co-workers with a resounding applause and congratulations. After an hour of partying, I walked to my office. I had a stack of folders on my desk that June had placed that morning. I opened the top folder, read it thoroughly and picked up the phone to call the parents of a child who was afraid to go to school. I thumbed through the rest of the folders, prioritized them and started the support process. I knew the months ahead would be difficult at times yet rewarding also.

Latisha was welcomed with the same greeting at her workplace. She had an equal number of cases and she accepted the challenge enthusiastically. Within a couple of months, I noticed that Latisha was quiet and sullen most of the time. I confronted her and asked what was bothering her? She said, "My caseload is overwhelming, and I am getting too personally involved in each." I asked, "Have you talked to your therapist?" She responded, "Yes, and she increased my depression medication. She wants to see if the increase helps, and if not, decide on other options," she said.

Latisha took the medication and attended therapy for the next three months. There was no change in her mental state. She got behind in her work, and frequently could not get out of bed in the morning. Finally, her supervisor recommended she take some time off. Latisha was reluctant but realized that her work performance had declined and that her emotional well-being was jeopardized. I picked her up on her last day of work. She got into the car, body trembling and tears in her eyes.

When we arrived home, she told me that her therapist had recommended that she be admitted to a mental health facility to treat her severe depression, stress, and anxiety. Latisha self-admitted herself to the Chicago Mental Health Hospital. She was tested and clinically diagnosed with a nervous breakdown. In addition to trembling and crying, Latisha exhibited a rapid heartbeat, shortness of breath and dizziness. The psychiatrist explained the treatment plan to us. It included exercising regularly, practicing relaxation techniques, counseling for stress, medication, getting enough sleep and a possible lifestyle modification. I asked, "Based on your experience, how successful are the treatment plans?" He informed us that if all went well, Latisha could be stabilized in a few days and the total stay could be from ten to fifteen days. He said that full recovery was possible if therapy, medication and coping strategies like exercise, fresh air, talking to a close friend and meditation or yoga were part of her daily life. [29]

Latisha and I left the doctor's office and returned to her hospital room. We both were familiar with treatment plans and the potential success they offered. We agreed to work together on the plan in the hospital and when she was released. Within eleven days, Latisha had successfully completed her treatment and was approved for self-release. She had significantly decreased all her symptoms and was ready to begin her home treatment plan. I decided to stay at home with her for a few days until she had established a routine.

The impact that Latisha's nervous breakdown had on me was devastating. I thought that her mental state was caused by getting married so quickly, my spending too much time at work or something more personal. I discussed my feelings with Latisha. She admitted that her nervous condition could be attributed to her passion, sensitivity, and the empathy she had for the families and children she supported and helped. She felt overwhelmed with her quantity of cases and her responsibilities. She was convinced that her involvement with clients was the direct cause. She felt that giving up her work would be the best alternative to modifying her lifestyle. We agreed to follow the home treatment plan and make the decision about her career another time.

Interlude Three

I had written seven chapters since Latisha's last update. She had asked occasionally how I was progressing with the novel, and I would respond, "Good." I had just closed the cover of my laptop and she appeared. I asked, "Do you have time to catch up on my writing progress?" She said, "I've been waiting patiently."

I began with a description of the presidential election of Jimmy Carter. I told her that Carter had a great platform that emphasized the importance of supporting the poor. He didn't accomplish a lot of what he proposed because he was a one-term president. I identified with his efforts and decided to compare him with other presidents in respect to poverty issues.

I told her that I wrote about my counselor responsibilities at the alternative program and, of course, the shooting. She wanted to discuss the shooting and the effect it had on my desire to help children. I told her that it reinforced my goals to help poor families and children with counseling support and resources.

Latisha was aware of the update section of the novel. She emphasized the importance of informing readers about my family and friends. She commented, "Too often, authors neglect giving updates on minor characters who play important roles in developing the main character."

I discussed the chapter about leaving the alternative program and accepting a counseling position at CCCS. I told her that my role as a counselor, supervising counselor and researcher had motivated me to possibly study psychology.

The final chapter of the update was my visit with Jimmy at the correction facility. I told Latisha that I had planned on going to the jail but put it off year after year. She spoke, "I know that the car accident and Janelle's death bothered you and the closure you needed was the visit." I responded, "You are right and telling Jimmy I that I forgave him might influence his future."

Latisha got up from her chair and said, "Thanks for the update. I like hearing how you have progressed from chapter to chapter." I responded, "I'm fortunate to have a sounding board who offers encouragement." She walked toward the kitchen, turned, and said, "Supper in an hour."

PART IV

CHAPTER 24

RESEARCH PROPOSAL

After my visit with Jimmy, I was eager to begin writing my research intervention proposal for June. My focus was generational poverty. My personal experience with situational poverty occurred when my father died. He and my mother both worked, and their income was above the current poverty level for a family of four. When my father died my mother's income fell well below the poverty level. As a result, we were forced to move into lower income housing in a segregated section of south Chicago. We lived in a project with hundreds of other poor families and attended poverty-level segregated schools. My mother and I worked hard for two years and were able to earn a higher income. After two years, we moved from the segregated project and schools to an apartment in an integrated neighborhood. We were fortunate the experience was short term. Our family did not fall into the generational poverty category as did millions of families in the United States. Generational poverty was defined as two generations born in poverty. Most of the families that we lived with for two years met this definition.

Proposal

Goal: Develop a program to increase the percentage of families receiving social services from CCCS using evidence and social-based intervention programs.

Objective: Increase social services usage over a two-year period from 25 percent to 50 per cent.

Evidence based or social-based interventions includes income support, material aid, institutional placement, mental health services, in-home health services, supervision, education, transportation, housing, medical services, legal services, in-home assistance, socialization, nutrition, and childcare. [30]

Two groups from the south side of Chicago (Hide Park and Fuller Park) would be randomly chosen from survey data criteria. Details: The survey data would be obtained through mailings or phone calls. One group would receive interventions the other would not. Race would be identified. Each group must meet ten of the twelve criteria. The criteria include parent income, parenteducational attainment, single/dual parenting, employment, housing, social service support, health insurance, prenatal care, court placements, foster placements, juvenile detention placements and prison sentences. The criteria must be cumulative over a three-year period. [31]

Participation with the interventions would be determined in respect to the following criteria:

1. Income must be below $22,000 for a family of four.
2. Parent Education at least a high school (HS) diploma.
3. Single Parent (identify mother, father, or name another family member).
4. Employment at or below current minimum wage ($3.10 per hr.).
5. Housing (rent).
6. Social services support within the last three years.
7. Health insurance (none).
8. Prenatal care (none).
9. Educational court placement (at least one child or one parent).
10. Juvenile placement (at least one child or one parent).
11. Foster placement (at least one child or one parent).
12. Prison sentence (at least one child or one parent).

Survey Question...Please choose at least five interventions you think would help your family.

1. Income support.
2. Material aid.
3. Institutional placement.
4. Mental health services.
5. In-home health services.
6. Supervision.
7. Education.
8. Transportation.
9. Housing.
10. Medical services.
11. Legal services.
12. In-home assistance.
13. Socialization.
14. Nutrition.
15. Childcare.

I finished writing my research proposal and made an appointment with June. Her secretary said she was out of the office until Friday. I asked if she had an opening to meet with me to review my proposal. Her secretary asked, “How’s three o’clock?” I said, “Fine.” I gave June’s secretary a copy of my proposal and asked that she give it to her.

June called when she returned, and we met to discuss the proposal. She was interested in pursuing the study and wanted me to make a presentation to the counseling team. I said that I would. She questioned variables like participant drug or alcohol addiction and mental health status. She recommended that if the study were approved; then I should make a statement about the variables.

I met with the team two days later. I was prepared to answer questions from the group. There were a few clarifications and concerns, but otherwise the counselors were supportive and recommended approval. I thanked them and began working on the project. June advised me that her expectation of working on the twenty cases assigned each month was included in my duties. I doubted could I find the time and help to do both? I recalled the support that Latisha had given me in a couple of cases. Maybe, she would help with the study.

When I got home, I told Latisha that my research study was approved, but I was concerned that I wouldn't be able to keep up with my caseload and complete the study. She responded, "How about I help you." I said, "I was hoping you would." She asked, "What are friends for?" I spoke, "You are more than a friend; you are my soulmate." I explained the study to her. She agreed to help with participant involvement.

We worked on the study for three months. Two hundred twenty-two families met the criteria, and they selected at least five service supports. We divided the total into two groups. Group A received the interventions and Group B did not. Group B was told that there were two groups and their interventions would start when the other group finished their two-year period. At the end of the two-year period, we hoped that at least fifty percent of Group A would continue to receive the interventions.

I continued working on cases assigned along with the study for the next four years. I was successful with providing support for most of the cases during that period. Group A completed their interventions after two years and fifty percent of the participating families continued receiving services. Group B was given their interventions for the next two-years. At the end of the two years, only thirty percent of the participating Group B families continued receiving services. I thought that the two-year wait influenced the results. Because the initial study was a preliminary, study another long-term study was needed to analyze which interventions were helpful in increasing services to reduce generational poverty.

Latisha and I worked diligently on the study for the four years. Our mutual support solidified our marriage. I was always concerned that the research project would be overwhelming and affect her mental health. I was pleased that it did not.

CHAPTER 25
NEW JOB

Latisha's illness was in my thoughts throughout the workday. I worried about her recovery and her future social service career. I recognized that she might not be able to assume her social work responsibilities, and a modification and adjustment in her personal life might be needed.

Despite my concern, I accomplished my daily responsibilities at CCCS. I continued to manage my caseload and provided as much support as possible to families and children. My coworkers were available and offered help if needed. June was incredibly supportive and advised me that if I needed time with Latisha, that other counselors would be available to pick up my cases.

The weeks and months passed, and Latisha was on the mend. She followed her treatment plan religiously and began to talk about returning to work. I noticed that her mental health had improved tremendously. She was like her old self. I wanted to encourage her return to work but feared that she would have a relapse. We talked about my concerns, and she assured me that she would return to work part time, reduce her caseload, and try not to become personally involved with her clients. Latisha was committed to her plan, and I was supportive. She returned to work after six months.

I was at my desk concentrating on a case and the phone rang; I answered. It was June. She asked if I could come to her office because she had received exciting news. I knocked on her door and walked in. She proceeded to inform me that she had been offered an executive position with CCCS and her position was available. She spoke, “I would like to recommend you for my position, would you be interested?” Her information and request were surprising. I hadn’t realized she was looking for an upper-level position, nor that she would consider me as her replacement. I told her I would give it some thought and discuss it with Latisha. I asked, “When do you need an answer?” “How about a week?” she responded.

Latisha had been back to work for a month and seemed to be back on track. Her part-time position and reduced caseload were manageable. I worried that a management position would require more work time, and it would influence her progress. When I arrived home that evening, Latisha was preparing supper, listening to her favorite music, and sipping a glass of wine. She looked incredibly happy.

I approached her and gave her a kiss on the cheek. I said, “You sure are in your element.” She spoke, “I had a great day at work, and I feel that I have recovered fully from my breakdown.” “That’s great!” I spoke. “I have some work news.” I spoke. “What?” she inquired. “June is taking a new position, and she offered her supervisor job to me,” I said. “That’s incredible,” she spoke. “And what did you say?” I told her I wanted to tell you first and get your opinion. Latisha said, “you have mine…go for it.” I was elated that Latisha was so supportive. My decision was made. I was going to become the supervising counselor for CCCS.

When I arrived at work the next day, rather than go to my office, I went straight to June’s office. I knocked and said, “I’m in.” She responded, “Great!”

Three months passed, and I had settled into my new job. My counseling team was working well, and I felt that they trusted my decisions and were supportive of my leadership. I considered resurrecting my previous internship research, which I felt was incomplete. My initial goal was to develop a program to increase the percentage of families receiving social services from CCCS using evidence and social-based intervention programs. The objective was to increase social services usage over a two-year period from

25 percent to 50 percent. I had achieved that goal with one group but not the other. I had initially selected two groups from the same geographic area (Hyde Park and Fuller Park). The Hyde Park group had received an array of interventions and was successful in continuing to receive support services. The Fuller Park group did not receive interventions and was not successful in receiving support. I felt concerned that the Fuller Park group did not meet the research goal and objectives. I decided to develop a new study for Fuller Park. I decided to review the initial research to see how the Hyde Park group was progressing and which services were being used.

The initial survey question asked participants to choose at least five interventions that would help their family, like income support, material aid, institutional placement, mental health services, in-home health services, supervision, education, transportation, housing, medical services, legal services, in-home assistance, socialization, nutrition, and childcare.

I analyzed the initial research data to determine which interventions were selected more often by participants and determine if poverty had been reduced over a five-year period. I found that income support, health services, education, housing, and childcare were selected by most participants. The five-year data results suggested that participants increased their incomes, became fully employed, improved their housing situation, participated in a health care program and accessed social services support more frequently. The current research results indicated that the study should be continued to determine which interventions helped reduce poverty from generation to generation.

I was pleased with the responsibilities of my new job and the results of the five-year study. Latisha continued working as a social worker and showed no stress or anxiety symptoms. We were happy and looked forward to helping more children and families.

CHAPTER 26

FOSTER KIDS

Latisha and I had been married for four years. She was doing well after her breakdown and her job was gratifying. I was pleased with my work but felt something was missing. We worked each day with families and children, and we had none of our own. Latisha also felt there was a void in our marriage. We had decided two years ago not to have children but wanted the experience of having a family. After careful consideration and a lot of thought we decided to foster two children. We understood the pros and cons and the difficulties foster children presented. Regardless, we decided to give it a try.

We understood the process and began filling out forms and other paperwork to qualify for a foster care program. We recognized that two people working in the social services field might have an advantage in getting approved. We completed the paperwork, submitted it to the foster agency and waited for their response. Within three weeks, we received a call requesting us to interview with an agency counselor. Latisha and I discussed the number of children we would like to foster, ages, race, and health factors. We knew that many foster children frequently moved from placement to placement for various reasons. Often those reasons boiled down to a poor foster parent match.

We met with the foster care counselor, and she reviewed our application. The foster placement committee approved our request as foster care parents. Latisha and I looked at each other and smiled. The counselor asked if we had given thought to the age group we would like to foster. We recognized that the older the child, the more baggage. We also knew that teen children were the most difficult to place. Before, we met with the counselor, Latisha and I decided that we would like to provide a home for two children in their early teens. We informed the counselor and she thumbed through a long list of possibilities. She asked, "Do you want to foster a boy or girl?" We had agreed that gender didn't matter. The counselor looked at us and said, "We have two thirteen-year-olds. Both are boys and have had numerous unsuccessful placements. The noticeable difference between the boys is that one was born into a family that experienced poverty for generations. The other boy lost his parents in a car accident four years ago, and struggles with mental health issues." Latisha and I looked at each other and immediately knew that we would accept both boys and give them as much love as possible. We signed all the documents and were told that we would receive a call to schedule a day and time to meet the boys.

We waited anxiously for the foster placement call. Finally, the phone rang on a Friday three weeks after we met with the counselor. I answered the phone immediately and recognized the counselor's voice. "Hello, Louis?" "Yes," I responded. She said that she had arranged separate meetings with the boys on Monday at three o'clock. I told her that we would be there. Latisha was overjoyed.

On Monday, we met with the counselor and Raul as scheduled. We were introduced to him, and he acknowledged us with a nod. Raul didn't say much during the interview but expressed his willingness to the placement. We met the second boy, Robert, an hour later. His personality was totally the opposite of Raul's. He was talkative and eager to be part of our family. After Robert left, the counselor told us that Raul had lived a life of generational poverty and Robert was raised in a well-to-do middle class family until his parents died in a car crash four years ago.

We picked the boys up from the foster care agency three days after the interview with them. The counselor said that she had introduced them to one another the day after the interview. They acted as though they had never met. The first meeting was awkward for them and us. Neither opened their mouths on the thirty-minute ride home. When we arrived home the boys carried their luggage into the apartment. They were to share the same bedroom. We gave them a tour and told them supper would be ready in a couple of hours. They walked to the bedroom and closed the door. Two hours later, I knocked on the door and said, "Supper is ready." The door opened immediately, and they walked toward the kitchen. Latisha asked the boys to take a seat told them what was on the menu. Latisha was a good cook, and she hoped that the boys liked what she had prepared. She served chicken tacos, a tossed salad and tortilla chips. The boys gobbled the tacos and chips but left the salad. Latisha and I asked the boys questions about their families during the meal and received one- or two-word responses," Yes ma'am, no sir." After dinner, I asked if they would like to watch a movie on TV. Both said, "Yes." I was surprised at their positive response. We watched a movie about a family moving from a city to a farm. I thought it was "corny," and I was certain the boys did too. It was ten o'clock and our bedtime. We said good night to them and watched them walk to their bedroom.

Latisha and I had taken the week off from work and got up early to make breakfast. The boys got up on their own and walked into the kitchen as we prepared the meal and placed it on the table. They were well dressed and seemed a bit friendly to one another.

They sat down for breakfast and gulped down the eggs, bacon, and toast we had prepared for them. I thought, "One thing for sure they like to eat." We asked what they would like to do? Both boys responded together and said, "Nothing." That was our cue to tell them that we had a plan. I told them we were taking a drive to the country, and they were coming with us.

We finished breakfast, cleaned up the kitchen, packed a few things, got in the car and drove off. Both boys had not volunteered to help with any of the road trip preparations. As we drove, I glanced in the rearview mirror and noticed that they looked disinterested and bored. We drove through the city and reached the country in an hour. Raul and Robert didn't say a word to each other or to us. Two hours later, we arrived at a cabin in a remote area. The cabin was surrounded by trees with a pond in sight. We unloaded the car and settled into the cabin. The boys did not help. Robert asked, "What's this all about?" I said, "We thought you would both like to get out of the city for a couple of days, so we rented this cabin. Robert said nothing. Raul walked off into the woods without a word.

Latisha and I unpacked food, bedding and cleaning supplies and placed them on the kitchen table. We settled into the cabin, got our fishing poles, and headed toward the pond. The boys were nowhere in sight. An hour had passed, and we saw both boys walking toward us. Robert said that he had never fished and asked if he could try. I responded, "Of course." He took the pole and cast the line, sat down, and waited for a bite. Raul walked over to Latisha and asked if he could try. She handed him the pole. We watched in amazement...had we found the "hook" we we're looking for? We walked back to the cabin to prepare lunch and occasionally glanced out the window. The boys were still there, and it looked like they were talking to each other.

The two days flew by and both boys seemed to get along. . .at least when we weren't looking. On the way home, we asked if they would like to take the trip again? They responded, "Yes." The following day we enrolled them in the neighborhood junior high school. They were both in eighth grade and were placed in the same class. We were apprehensive about how the boys would adjust. We waited at the door hoping that their first day was positive. Robert opened the door and Raul followed. Both boys walked to their room, closed the door, and came out when called to supper. Nothing was said the rest of the evening. Latisha and I had agreed that the boys would initiate communication with us on their own. We all went to bed at ten o'clock.

In the morning, Robert came into the kitchen and sat down. I asked, "Where's Raul?" Robert spoke, "He wasn't in his bed when I woke up." I ran to his room. He was gone! Robert went to school and Latisha, and I waited patiently for Raul's return. Robert came home from school and went to his room. At eight o'clock, Latisha and I decided to call the police. Raul had been missing for more than twenty-four hours. We both knew that the police would allow us to file a missing person's report after twenty-four hours. Latisha was about to pick up the phone when we heard a knock on the door. It was Raul. He came into the house, walked to his bedroom, and shut the door. We looked at each other and Latisha said, "We will deal with Raul in the morning." We went to bed.

The boys had been with us for five days. There was a limited amount of conversation with us and with each other. We began to question our desire to be foster parents. We decided that it was time to establish rules and determine if they would continue to stay with us. We called the boys into the living room and began the discussion. We realized that we had to be careful with our message. The experience we had in the social service field would be helpful.

The initial discussion was directed to Raul. I began, "Raul, we are pleased that you returned safely last night. We were worried and were going to call the police. We have decided that family rules need to be set. The first rule is to communicate where and when we are going someplace and that includes all of us." Raul spoke up and said he left because he didn't think the placement would work for him. He said, he walked the streets for hours and realized that he had nowhere to go...he was lost. He decided to give it another try, and he came back. Latisha told him that he made the right decision and that we would work together as a "family" to overcome future issues...rule number two.

Robert sat quietly listening to our discussion with Raul. I asked, "Robert would like to comment on the rules or anything else?" He said, "I am trying hard to adjust, but it is hard, because I don't think it will work." I assured him that if we all worked together there was a possibility, we could make it happen.

Rule three...we must learn to communicate. I began: "Raul, you, and Robert need to begin talking to one another instead of ignoring each other. We know it's hard because you don't know each other. Our advice...get to know each other. Also, if either one of you has a problem or concern, let's talk about it." Then I said, "The discussion we are having right now is a good example. In the future any one of us can call a meeting to talk about any issue or problem. Got it." I asked? Both boys nodded, "Yes." I said, "I can't hear you." They both verbalized, "Okay." Latisha asked, "Would you like to eat out for lunch?" Both boys raised their voices and said, "Yes, ma'am."

The boys walked to their room and we discussed their family history. Robert's parents had died in a car accident, and he had been shuffled among four different placements in four years. Prior to his parents' death he had lived in a secure white middle-class family setting. Their death was the underlying cause for his current behavior. Because his life changed drastically, he had difficulty adjusting to the placements. We knew that to help Robert we had to help him feel secure again.

Raul's family situation was completely different from Robert's. Raul was Hispanic and lived in poverty for years. His parents and grandparents lived a life of total insecurity for generations. He was abandoned and placed in foster care by his parents when he was eight years old. During those years, he was placed with six different families. None of them worked and he ran off from all the foster homes. We decided that despite his family situation, his greatest need was acceptance. He needed Latisha, Robert, and I to create a secure environment for him to gain confidence.

For the next four months, we worked hard at following the rules. There were blowups and angry moments, but we got through them. The family discussions offered a secure option to improve communication and make decisions. Additional rules were added and agreed to by all. The boys attended school every day and made average grades. There were no incidents requiring parent conferences or other behavior consequences at school or home. We were pleased with our efforts and realized that things could change at any time.

Latisha and I recognized that it was time for our family to live in a real house. We had saved enough for a down payment and decided to look in the Hyde Park area. We informed the boys of our plan and began the process. Both boys were excited about the prospect of living in a house with their own bedrooms and not being uprooted from their school. We found a suitable house in our price range within two months. We hired a moving van, packed our personal items and headed for a new adventure.

CHAPTER 27
MASTER'S DEGREE

Our family had been living together for two years. Robert and Raul were sophomores at Hyde Park High School. An academic program with an emphasis on a four-year college was not in their cards. They wanted to learn a skill or trade. Robert was interested in food services and Raul construction technology. There were a few vocational schools in Chicago that offered two-year trade programs. Latisha and I helped the boys apply to the schools and hoped that they were accepted.

The boys weren't the only members of our family interested in a new school. I decided that I would apply to the University of Chicago's Psychology (U of C's) program. I made an appointment to talk to the dean of psychology about my interest in applying to the program. I wanted to continue my research and expand it from a local level (Fuller Park, Chicago) to a state level (Illinois).

The beginning of a new school year and the fall semester at U of C was only two weeks away. The boys hadn't heard about their acceptance to the vocational school, and I hadn't heard if I was accepted into the psychology program. We all waited patiently for notification from the vocational school and university. After two days, Latisha called the vocational school and found out that both boys were accepted into their chosen programs and would be formally notified by mail. I decided to follow Latisha's lead and called the psychology dean. His receptionist took my name and telephone number and said she would give my message to the dean. The dean called the next day and asked if I would meet with him. I said, "Yes."

We met the following day. He informed me that I was accepted but wanted to review a few things before I started classes. He said that he had reviewed my application and resume and felt that I could complete the program in two years attending classes part time. He informed me that my internship would be waived because of previous internships at the alternative program and my work experience at CCCS. He asked questions about my research project. I told him I would like to use US census data to compare Illinois poverty percentages with other states during the 1980s and make recommendations to reduce poverty levels. He said, "sounds ambitious and the department will support your study with funds, personnel and technical support." I thanked him and walked out of his office overjoyed.

When I got home, I told everyone my good news. Latisha and the boys were excited for me. I said, "This calls for a celebration." We hopped in the car and went to our favorite restaurant. The boys and I had achieved our education goals and looked forward to the new school year.

The new school year started, and Latisha and I continued working. She as a part-time social worker, and I as the supervisor of counselors at CCCS. I attended evening classes and the boys immersed themselves in learning their trades.

Research Abstract

The study began with a Google search for researchers who studied Illinois poverty in the 1980s. I identified two authors who studied and published 1991 articles about poverty. The first study was written by Patricia Simpson and titled, "Trends in Illinois Poverty: 1979 to 1988." [32]

I learned that the 1980 poverty rates in Illinois and in the United States increased in contrast to the decreased rates in the 1960s and 1970s. The

1980s increase fell disproportionately on blacks. In Illinois, the poverty rate increased from 11 percent to 12.3 percent. Regionally, Chicago accounted for the largest concentration of poor Illinoisians. In 1988, sixty-six percent of the state's poor lived in the city. The poverty rates for whites, blacks, and Hispanics were 52, 75 and 93 percent, respectively.

The poverty growth among blacks increased more than whites and Hispanics. The black poverty rate was 30.2 percent in 1979 and rose to 37.9 in 1988. The increase was more than double the growth rates of whites and tripled the rate for Hispanics. Black poverty increases were attributed to a decrease in population, as well as to the income disparity between blacks and other ethnic and racial groups. [33]

The socioeconomic characteristics that influenced this disparity included the increase in the number of female-headed black families and unemployment. The decline of the two-parent family structure and composition influenced the opportunity for black males to earn enough money to sustain the responsibilities of fatherhood.

To combat the increase in poverty and breakdown in families requires government policies that target the needs of the poor to create job training and economic development strategies. Examples of job creations include options like grants, contracts, loans, and tax breaks. Another possible solution to increasing employment among the poor was skill training.

This study supported the work that I had been doing at CCCS for the past ten years. Most of the clients that elicited support were poor single-family black females who were unemployed and dependent on welfare for financial assistance. Their generational poverty situation affected their children educationally, emotionally, and psychologically. The support that counselors provided included social program information and assistance, school resource supports and family counseling. Social service workers recognized that financial and employment assistance were needed but not part of our social role.

The second study was written by Jon Javeman, Sheldon Danzier and Robert Plotnick. The article was titled, "State Poverty Rates for Whites, Blacks and Hispanics in the late 1980s." This study found that poverty rates in all states were extremely high. The US Bureau of the Census identified poverty lines as...family size, number of related children and the age of the household head which were used to compile the data. For example, the poverty line for a family of four was $12,092. Poverty rates were estimated by comparing the monetary income of a family to its corresponding poverty line. If the income was below the poverty line, then all the persons in that family were counted as poor. [34]

This Javeman, et.al. study looked at the Illinois poverty rate for Black Non-Hispanic and compared to other states located in the same geographic area. For example, the Illinois poverty rate for this group was (36.8). Other states that had comparable poverty rates located in the "Rust Belt' included Ohio (34.9), Indiana (32.0, Michigan (34.2) and Missouri (32.8). The mean family income for Illinois in the late 1980s was $37,939. The mean family incomes for Ohio ($35,044), Indiana ($32,175), Michigan ($37,218) and Missouri ($32,700), respectively. [35]

All five states located in the mid-western part of the US lost manufacturing jobs and unemployment increased. The loss of manufacturing jobs in the early 1980s corresponded with the recession and declining labor force. The disappearance of industrial jobs and businesses that supported them led to greater poverty for families and children. [36]

The high poverty rates and low mean family incomes in Illinois influenced all three ethnic groups but more significantly the Black Non-Hispanic population. Unemployment led to poverty and adversely affected families and children. The effects included strained relationships, poorer physical and mental health, reduced child development, health care loss, housing stress and increased education inequities. [37]

Because of the recession and declining labor force, the dominant governmental concerns were with fiscal restraint and major cutbacks in social programs. This restraint and cutbacks only exacerbated the poverty issue in Illinois and other manufacturing states.

The unemployment effect on poverty in Illinois and other "Rust Belt" states led to the role social service agencies would play in assisting and supporting families and children. Because agencies are limited in scope and finances their assistance is directed toward providing resource information and counseling support. Additionally, assistance with family management skills, child rearing and parenting programs are available. [38]

My personal exposure to poverty continued to surface as I pursued my research. I felt the poverty impact because I had lived it. Although it was situational, my experience continued to influence my goal to help families and children. I hoped that my study would contribute to the need for greater federal, state, and local support and assistance.

CHAPTER 28

UNIVERSITY OF CHICAGO

I continued working at CCCS until I completed my master's degree in psychology. The dean of psychology at the University of Chicago was pleased with my work experiences and the research I had done on the social services needs of poor blacks in the Fuller Park area of Chicago. The day that I received my degree, the dean offered me an Assistant Clinical Professorship position. I was spellbound. He believed that I would make a positive addition to the faculty. I hadn't given any thought to teaching or doing research at the University level. It was a tremendous opportunity, and one that I accepted without reservation.

I had no idea the dean would offer the faculty position, so my news was a complete surprise to Latisha, Robert, and Raul. When I told them the news, they were thrilled for me. Raul said, "This calls for a celebration." We readied ourselves and drove to one of our favorite restaurants. The boys always loved good news because it gave them an opportunity to participate as a family. Something they had lost sight of for many years.

The next step for me was to resign from CCCS. I called June and informed her of my good fortune. She expressed her gratitude for my work and wished me well. I called a meeting with the counselors and told them about my new position. Upon hearing the news, they stood up and clapped joyously.

I had worked at CCCS for ten years. First, as a counselor and then a counselor supervisor. I had enjoyed my work there, especially the opportunity to do research on the social services needs of blacks living in poverty. I felt that the faculty position at the University of Chicago would enable me to use the data I compiled for my master's thesis to continue researching and teach courses about the importance of collecting data to identify the needs of people living in poverty. I also felt that the position would allow me to conduct field work and compile data to conduct poverty studies.

I gave a two week's notice to CCCS and started my new job on the Tuesday after Labor Day. The dean had chosen an office for me, and I settled in quickly. A faculty meeting had been called for ten o'clock, and I was the first one in the room. I was introduced to the faculty and asked to give some background information and future goals. They were pleased with my responses and expressed their availability for assistance.

I was given two research introductory courses to teach to incoming freshmen. I thought it was a great opportunity to express the importance of collecting data to study the needs of people in poverty. The position also afforded me the opportunity to continue to conduct research and study the social service resources and supports available from the federal, state, and local governments.

I was also excited about going into the "field" to find out what and how public assistance would benefit the poor. I realized that identifying needs was important, but poor families and children needed an option to access support. My first thought was to start a clinic at the university. I recognized that the University couldn't go it alone. First, there was no money, staff or facility. I decided that to achieve the clinic goals, partners were needed. The dean had mentioned his support for the project, the faculty had offered their assistance and public agencies like CCCS and Chicago social service agencies were likely partners to start the clinic.

Two months had passed and the two research courses I was teaching prompted six students t to help with my research, field work and the start-up clinic. I was thrilled that my beliefs could influence undergrads to volunteer their services. Our "team" met one afternoon to devise a plan to accomplish three objectives. Two of the students agreed to work on identifying resources and support for clinic participants. Two would accompany me on my field work and the final two would work in the clinic. The work began in the second semester. The research group reviewed literature, compiled data and submitted a proposal to identify what the clinic could do to provide resources and support for poor families and children. Their research identified the need to increase wages, receive earned income tax credit, utilize evidence-based family and social-based prevention programs, public investments in parental care, outside interventions from the private sector,education, job training, health insurance, Medicaid, nutrition programs and food support.

The data that the research team identified helped me with my research objectives. Their work provided the "needs" of families and children living in poverty. I needed specific data that would identify the numbers and percentages of the Chicago population that needed resources and support.

To determine the number and percentage need, our group knocked on doors, visited churches, attended meetings and talked to agencies, schools, government entities and many other options. The need for data was overwhelming. We found that the number of families and children needing resources and support was fifty-five percent. The number suggested that a majority of the Chicago population could benefit from a walk-in clinic housed at the University of Chicago in the Hyde Park area.

I made an appointment with the dean and gathered our team to make a presentation. We explained resource and support research, needs data and the percentage of families and children expressing their support for a clinic. The dean listened attentively, asked several questions and gave his approval. I contacted CCCS, two other service agencies, faculty and asked for their assistance. I described the goals and objectives of the clinic. All were supportive and offered to volunteer. The team was thrilled and began identifying what was needed to open the clinic.

CHAPTER 29

FAMILY UPDATE

My life had progressed well. Latisha was working part time and had modified her lifestyle so that there was less work stress. Raul and Robert had graduated from vocational school and we're working in the trades they chose. My brother, Peter, continued to work at Radio Shack, and moved his family from the city to the suburbs. Mindy had married and she lived on the South Side. She had one child and worked at Chicago Med as an emergency nurse. Rosie was unmarried, lived in Lincoln Park and taught high school English at Hyde Park High School.

My mother had retired from the meat packing plant for two years. She lived alone in the house my brother and I bought for her after my father died, when we had moved from the projects. She had been diagnosed with breast cancer and had weekly chemo and radiation treatments. The doctors said that her cancer was stage four and remission, or a cure were unlikely.

Robert had met his partner while interning at a local restaurant. His partner's father owned the restaurant and hired Robert after he graduated. Robert had been working at the restaurant for two years and recently moved into his partner's apartment located in the heart of the city. The restaurant was successful, and he enjoyed his job and his relationship.

Raul had found a construction job with a heavy equipment company. He had learned how to operate a crane and was extremely competent at it. He enjoyed the bachelor life and his work. He had successfully removed himself from family generational poverty and had no intentions of returning to a life of poverty.

Mindy loved her work as a nurse. She enjoyed the trauma of the emergency room and was often sought by other hospitals. Her daughter, Lynn, was in preschool and quite close to me. I saw her as much as I could. She called me her favorite uncle. Mindy's husband was a physician and had a family practice on the South Side.

Rosie was recognized at Hyde Park High School for her excellent teaching skills. She was extremely popular with the students who lived in poverty. I believe she acquired her empathy from the time we lived in Fuller Park. Living in the projects and attending a segregated junior high afforded her experiences that she brought to the teaching profession. When I finished my novel, I hoped that Rosie would help with editing.

I was extremely proud of my brother and sisters. I was especially gratified that Mindy and Rosie had chosen service professions. Latisha often commented that I had influenced their professional career choices. I was overly concerned with my mother's health, and hoped she would continue her battle against cancer.

CHAPTER 30

SEPTEMBER 11, 2001

I arrived at work about fifteen minutes late that infamous Tuesday morning. My office desk clock read 9:00 AM. I walked out of my office and opened the lunchroom door. A group of clinic volunteers were gathered around a small TV. The look on their faces was frightening. As I approached the group, I heard the TV reporter scream in horror, "The south side of the World Trade Center Towers has been hit by another airplane." I couldn't believe what I heard. I looked for someone to tell me what happened. Jeanie, a student volunteer, explained that an airplane had struck the north side of the towers at 8:46 AM and the south side at 9:03 AM. I turned my head toward the TV and listened to the reporter. [39]

I listened intently as she described what had happened and explained the known details. I glanced at the wall clock and noticed it was 9:15 AM. The volunteers and I were glued to the TV waiting for more information. We were all mesmerized and in shock. By mid-afternoon, authorities had gathered information and began reporting what was known. CNN reported that nineteen men hijacked four fuel-loaded US commercial airplanes bound to west coast destinations. A total of 2,977 people were killed at the World Trade Center in New York City, at the Pentagon in Washington, DC and in a remote field outside of Shanksville, Pennsylvania. [40]

An exhaustive investigation was undertaken by the US government, state, and local agencies and police forces. The investigation found that an Islamic extremist terrorist group called "Al Qaeda" was responsible for all three of the coordinated attacks. The leader of the Islamic group Osama bin Laden was found to be the mastermind. He went into hiding for ten years. On May 2011, US Navy Seals launched an attack on his compound in Pakistan killing the Al Qaeda leader. [41]

Americans and world leaders were shocked that the terrorists were able to penetrate US airport security and accomplish the attack. America had let its guard down and thousands were killed and hundreds of thousands felt the impact of 9/11 at the time and for years later.

To prevent a future terrorist attack the federal government created the Transportation Security Administration (TSA) in November 2001 and the Homeland Security Department in March 2002. Both federal agencies assumed the responsibility of preventing another terrorist attack on America. [42]

The effect of the terrorist attack on poor children and families was unpublized. I researched its effects and found nothing. The business community was primarily concerned because the stock market plummeted. However, the markets bounced back in a relatively short time. My family and I were unscathed because we lived in Chicago. For some laborers and service workers living in the NYC region, the loss of jobs and wages must have been felt in some poor households.

The terrorist attack has become an indelible American catastrophe that is remembered every year since the attack. Americans recognized the twentieth anniversary in 2021.

CHAPTER 31

NEIGHBORHOOD RETURN

I hadn't returned to the Fuller Park neighborhood in nearly twenty-five years. All the work and educational experiences I had since living in the projects and attending a segregated school played a huge part in my passion to help families and children in poverty.

I decided to ask Mindy and Rosie to accompany me to the old neighborhood. They had often expressed their desire to see where we lived and the school they attended for two years. We frequently talked about our short-term poverty situation and their desire to help poor people.

We met at Hyde Park High School one fall Saturday morning. We climbed into my car and started our journey. We drove down Hyde Park Boulevard and commented on the changes from block to block. We arrived at 47th street and area 37 of Chicago's 77 community areas and read the The sign, "Welcome to Fuller Park" The Park was named after a Chicago attorney and Chief Justice of the United States, Melville Weston Fuller who served between 1988 and 1910. [43]

It had been a home to lower classes throughout its history. It was considered one of the worst areas of the city because of its high rates of crime and violence. Its population had declined from year to year since we lived there in 1966. The area maintained its 90 percent black population since its inception. The white population began to decrease in the '70s when "white flight" was at its peak. As years passed the area became more populated with Hispanics and fewer whites. [44]

In 1930, the area was named "Bronzeville" by James Gentry, a theater editor for the Chicago Bee. He said that African-Americans' skin color was closer to bronze than black. The name was popularized by the Chicago Defender, a black newspaper with nationwide circulation.

Bronzeville was well known for its nightclubs and dance halls...but fell into decline after the end of racially restricted housing. Upper and middle-class families moved away, and over-population and poverty overwhelmed the neighborhood. [45]

As we drove, we looked for the schools we attended. The junior high had been consolidated with another and no longer existed. We passed DuSable High School and learned that it was identified as "Bronzeville Scholastic Institute and the Williams Prep School of Medicine."

We continued our Saturday morning journey and headed toward the neighborhood we lived in before our move to the projects. We drove down 55th street and found our old house. The front yard was well kept; it had a new paint job and the driveway was replaced recently. Our family's first home brought back good and bad memories. I recalled joyous holidays, birthday parties and game night. I visualized my father's body lying on the grass next to the newly poured concrete driveway and my mother's screams of remorse coming from the living room. It was an unpleasant memory that haunted me throughout my life. I took a couple of pictures of the house and pulled away from the curb.

Mindy, Rosie, and I shared a tear or two and continued our drive. We drove north on Hyde Park Boulevard and reached the retail and restaurant section of town. The streets were crowded and live music was heard from block to block. We parked our car and walked toward the busy Boulevard. It was nearly noon, and we decided to have lunch. We found a small outdoor restaurant and ordered lunch. Mindy had a waffle with chicken. Rosie and I ordered catfish, fries and slaw. The food was delicious. After lunch we looked into a couple of stores and headed toward the parking lot. Just before we got to our car, I noticed an ice cream store. I couldn't pass it up. I walked in and bought a cup of vanilla mixed berry special. As we approached the parking lot, three women walked toward me. One stepped closer and asked, "What kind of ice cream do you have?" I said, "I don't know the name." She looked into the cup and said, "Cheesecake." I asked, "How did you know?" She responded, "It's my favorite."

We hopped in our car and drove toward Michigan Avenue and headed to Hyde Park High School. Because Rosie taught English at the school, she was familiar with the curriculum and student population. She said that the courses taught varied from general, advanced to baccalaureate options. The student population was 99 percent black and lived within the Woodlawn area. I had driven past the high school many times because it was located near the University of Chicago. Before leaving, I stepped out of the car and took a couple of pictures. Its new name was "Hyde Park Academy High School." Mindy, Rosie, and I hugged one another, said goodbye and I thanked them for a great day. They walked to their car, and I jumped into mine and drove home.

When I got home, I found Latisha in the living room reading one of her favorite mysteries. She asked, "How was your trip with your sisters down memory lane?" I sensed a tinge of jealousy in the tone of her voice. I said, "I enjoyed seeing the high school and neighborhood I grew up in after my father died. We also drove by the project area we lived in for two years. We ate lunch in an outdoor restaurant and took a peek at Hyde Park High where Rosie taught English. It was fun being with my sisters and reminiscing." Latisha commented, "Let's take the same tour in a couple of weeks. I would love to see the old neighborhood too." "Great idea, I would like to find out what a couple of my boyhood friends are doing," I responded.

Two weeks had passed, and we decided we would take a Sunday afternoon drive. It was a beautiful day to take a tour of my boyhood neighborhood. It would also give us an opportunity to see my mother. We began our tour with a drive past DuShane High School and the projects. Latisha remarked, "The projects are gone and replaced with vacant lots." I said, "Yes, they were torn down years ago and the area has become an eyesore."

We drove north toward the University of Chicago and the street we lived on before moving to the projects. We pulled alongside our old house, and I noticed a familiar face mowing the lawn across the street. I got out of the car and walked over to the mower. It was Pauly. One of my best friends. I hadn't seen him in more than twenty-five years. We had lost track of one another when I moved to the projects. We greeted each other with a hug, asked each other how we were doing and began to talk about the old days…school, baseball, chestnut challenges. I introduced him to Latisha, and he invited us into his house to meet his wife and children. His wife, Peg, was waiting at the front door with his four children. We were introduced, sat down and sipped our iced tea. We continued our conversation about our boyhood experiences. I asked, "How's Johnny doing?" Pauly said, "Unfortunately he had cancer and died two years ago. "How sad," I said. We visited for another hour and thanked Pauly and Peg for their hospitality.

We walked to our car, got in and headed toward my mother's house. When we arrived, we walked toward the front door. I sensed that something wasn't right…the front window curtains were closed and the porch light was on. I looked at Latisha and said, "The curtains are never closed and the porch light is on." I knocked on the door and my mother did not answer. "Louis, the neighbor next door," yelled. "Rosie had an ambulance take your mother to the hospital." "Do you know what happened?" I asked. "I am not sure; she was conscious when the EMTs put her in the ambulance, the neighbor responded. "Do you know which hospital they took her to?" I asked. She responded, "Mercy."

Latisha and I bolted to the car, and I drove as fast as allowed. When we arrived at the hospital, I asked the receptionist which room Mrs. Van Patton was in. She said, "206." When I got to the room, Peter, Rosie, and Mindy were at my mother's bedside. I looked at my mother, she looked white, frail, and weak. I greeted my brother and sisters and approached my mother's bed. She looked up at me and said, "Doesn't look good…does it?" She slipped into unconsciousness. I didn't respond. I heard a knock on the door and the doctor walked in. He looked at the four of us and said, "The tests indicate that your mother had a stroke…it was minor…but it was compounded by the fact that your mother's cancer has reached stage five." We looked at him in horror. We knew our next question was, "How long does she have?" He looked at my mother and said, "I am not sure she will regain consciousness." We stood by my mother's bed through the night. In the morning, we watched the sun peek through the blinds as it reflected off my mother's face. She had passed. We were fortunate to see her before she died, and in our own way said, "Goodbye." My mother and I were remarkably close especially after my father died and we moved to the projects. She was strong and resilient. I knew I would miss her dearly.

My brother, sisters and I planned her funeral. We knew she believed in a traditional model, so we contacted a funeral director and consulted with her as she prepared my mother's wake and burial. We invited all our friends and my mother's girlfriends. I asked Pauly and his wife, Floyd, Jill, Steve and Sheila if they would like to come to the funeral. They all accepted. It meant a lot to me…they were my closest friends. Days and months past, and I resumed my daily responsibilities at the University. When not concentrating on my work, my thoughts were always about my mother.

HYDE PARK HOUSE, 2021

PROJECTS, 2021

Hyde Park High School, 2021

DuSable High School, 2021

Interlude Four

Much had transpired in the past eight years...New Job, Foster Kids, Master's Degree, University of Chicago Job, Family Update and Neighborhood Return. I sat back on my chair and reminisced about each experience.

My head came out of the clouds, and I heard a familiar voice. "Time for supper," Latisha yelled. I got up from my chair and sauntered to the kitchen. Latisha was placing food on the table and humming one of her favorite melodies. I sat down and filled my plate with one of her specialties...pork chops, sweet potatoes, and green beans. Latisha sat down beside me and asked, "What's new with your novel?" She knew I had been working on it all day, and I was dying to give her an update. "Oh nothing, samo old samo," I said, jokingly.

While eating, we talked about my supervisory position with CCCS. I was proud of my work, because it gave me an opportunity to function in a management position and develop a much-needed research project to determine the social service needs of families in the community. My current assistant professor position at the University of Chicago was exciting and challenging. I was able to continue to do research, teach students and develop a walk-in/outreach clinic. Latisha asked a couple of questions about my work and the clinic. She was especially interested in the services that the clinic would provide to the South Side community.

We talked about the happiness fostering Robert and Raul had given us. They had given us so much pleasure and contributed to having a family to care for and love. Just like any other family we had our ups and downs but were able to maintain a family unit despite our age and the needs of two teenage boys from two totally different environments. We had accepted the challenge and dealt with rocks in the road as they surfaced. We were pleased with their growth and progress.

The family update had always been special for both of us. I told Latisha that the return to the old neighborhood helped me realized that all families need each other and as much support as possible. I said that I was more pleased about her return to work than anything that had happened since our last discussion. I mentioned that I was very happy that she was able to continue her passion helping families and children. She responded, "So am I, my work is important to me personally, but more importantly I am contributing to our community."

I continued expressing my thoughts and finally said to Latisha, "I really don't think that I would have been as successful with work and school without your support and encouragement." "Thank you, we do make a good team," Latisha spoke. With that said, we finished our supper, watched TV and went to bed anxious to start another day.

PART V

The Clinic

Food and Nutrition

KIDS Count

Presidents and Poverty

Retirement

Donald J. Trump

COVID – 19

Joe Biden

January 6, 2021

Equity and Equality

Family/Friend Recap - 2021

Conclusion

Interlude Five

Epilogue

Post Preface

CHAPTER 32

THE CLINIC

I had been working at the University of Chicago for three years teaching introductory research classes and managing the walk-in/reach-out poverty clinic. My students were receptive to the content taught and extremely praiseworthy of my instructional style. I was always gratified when I received my semester evaluations from them. Many of the students volunteered to work in the clinic when they completed the courses. It felt like I was making a difference and guiding them toward their career goals.

By 1994, the clinic had expanded its services and resources. Initially, it was primarily a corner walk-in option for local residents. As word spread, the clinic's monthly participation numbers increased from fifty to well over one hundred walk-ins.

The volunteers included students, my family, friends, social service workers, and University faculty. Our volunteers were especially proud of our family education programs. We offered GED classes, prenatal care, teen pregnancy for both parents, head start, employment preparation, and job awareness. Additionally, the clinic provided referral, consultation, counseling and therapy for families and children.

Resources included information, guidance, and support for federal, state and local programs. Brochures, pamphlets, and other printed information were available for pick up and explanation. Information about eligibility, income limits and US citizen requirements were explained. A referral system was in place for clients to contact human service or social service agencies for more support.

Information on federally supported programs for state implementation, design, type and the amount of assistance, including food, healthcare, housing, and financial poverty options. Walk-in resources and support included information about how to apply and eligibility. Information offered to clients was identified and explained in detail. We were especially aware clients did not understand the specifics of each program and were often fearful of applying. Our volunteers took great pains to make sure clients understood and to address their fears. Each of us was schooled on the details of the programs and how to help clients apply. The programs included the following.

Food

SNAP '33 (Supplemental Nutrition Assistance Program) is based on monthly income. The program aids needy families so that children may be cared for in their own home or in a home of relatives. [46]

WIC '74 (Women, Infants and Children) is a special supplemental nutrition program for women, infants, and children to end dependency of needy parents on government benefits by promoting job preparation, work, and marriage. It is designed to prevent and reduce the incidence of out-of-wedlock pregnancies and to reduce incidents of abuse . It encourages the formation and maintenance of two-parent families· [47]

TANF '96 (Temporary Assistance for Needy Families) offers cash assistance to needy families so that children may remain in their own homes, reducing the dependency of needy parents by promoting job preparation, work, and marriage; preventing out-of-wedlock pregnancies; and encouraging the formation and maintenance of two-parent families. The eligibility requirements include being unemployed or underemployed and having extremely low income. The help also includes childcare, job training and food, clothing, and housing support. [48]

Health Care

Medicaid '65 is a federal government sponsored medical insurance program for states. It provides help for low-income adults and their children with limited incomes. [49]

CHIP '97 (Children's Health Insurance Program) provides federal matching funds to states to provide health coverage to children in families with incomes too high to qualify for Medicaid, but who can't afford private coverage. [50]

Housing

HUD '65 (Housing and Urban Development) is a program designed for families to receive subsidized housing and housing vouchers. The program helps low-income families get into affordable private or government owned rental housing. [51]

LIHEAP '81 (Low Income Home Energy Assistance Program) helps low-income households pay for heating and cooling bills and offers low-cost home improvements. [52]

Financial Assistance

AFDC '36 (Aid to Families with Dependent Children) provides grants to states to provide cash welfare programs for needy children who have been deprived of parental support or care because their father or mother was absent from home, incapacitated or deceased. [53]

SSI '35 (Supplemental Social Security Income) provides cash to low-income seniors and low-income adults and kids with disabilities. [54]

I frequently reminded myself of the two years our family lived in the projects. My mother had not sought any federal or state poverty assistance. She certainly qualified financially. Maybe she was unaware of the programs or too proud to apply. Regardless, her income and my support enabled our family to overcome the situation and progress with our lives. The clinic's education, counseling, and resource/support programs continued to grow. In 1997, we decided to create an out-reach program. We realized that many needy families could not take advantage of the walk-in program but would access resources and services in neighborhood churches, schools and community centers.

Our first experience in the out-reach program occurred in our evening school option. We advertised services in local neighborhood stores, church rectories and community athletic centers. We opened our doors at seven o'clock and found a long line of people waiting. We had five volunteers and before long each had four families waiting in line for their help.

My first family had questions about LIHEAP (Low Income Home Energy Assistance). An elderly lady with a confused expression stood before me with three children under the ages of eight years. She explained that her daughter had left the children with her without money. Her major concern was to keep the children warm during the upcoming winter. I told her about LIHEAP and based on her poverty level, she would qualify for assistance. I asked a few more questions and told her that she should apply for the AFDC (Aid to Families with Dependent Children) program. I asked one of the counselors to help her apply for both programs. She thanked me for my help and walked away with the three children in tow with a smile on her face.

Next in line was a teenager carrying an infant. I asked her how I could help, and she spoke that she was worried about good food for her baby. She had no job or money to buy formula or baby food. I asked a few more questions and told her about the WIC (Women, Infants and Children) program. I explained that it was a special supplemental nutrition program for women, infants and children. She was excited about the program and asked how to apply. One of the student volunteers approached and escorted her to a table to help with her application.

The night had gone by quickly and our team had helped more than thirty families and children with information to help them with their poverty issues. I felt great and realized that reaching out to local neighborhoods and offering walk-in support and resources at the clinic were a double-edged sword that would sharpen itself as the years passed.

CHAPTER 33

FOOD AND NUTRITION

The walk-in and out-reach programs at the clinic continued to grow and our team felt that a positive effect on poverty had been made in many of the neighborhoods. An issue that continued to surface time and again was the lack of healthy food and nutrition. I decided to learn more about others who were active in addressing food and nutrition needs. And I identified the Greater Chicago Food Depository.

The program had opened in 1979 at Robert Strube's produce stall in the South Water Market He and his friends decided to find a more systematic way of feeding people experiencing hunger in Chicago and Cook County. They began distributing food with virtually nothing…it became a twelve-hour day and seven days a week. Its founders started with a cadre of volunteer workers who helped raise money and solicit food donations. [55]

Within six years (1986) the program had moved to a permanent location on the south side of Chicago and started a perishable food program called "Food Rescue." The program collected unused, but edible, food from grocery stores for distribution to food pantries and soup kitchens. Between 1993 and 1998, hot meals were served to after-school programs and the Chicago Community Kitchen offered culinary and job training for unemployed and underemployed adults.

From 2000 to 2006, the farmer's market on wheels was started for low-income communities, the "Pantry University" was initiated as a training program for staff and volunteers from member agencies and a program for children and older adults were developed.

In 2009 and 2010, a benefit outreach program was started to help eligible individuals in applying for federal nutrition benefits. Between 2010 and 2012, the children's program expanded with a healthy kid's initiative for schools and a summer lunch bus meal distribution at community sites.

The Chicago Food Depository continued expanding from 2012 and 2018. A veteran's outreach program was established, partnerships with community health agencies were forged and a food security program for adults with disabilities were founded. Today, the Depository services include seven hundred Chicago pantries, soup kitchens and shelters.

My research led to a plan to establish a partnership between the clinic and the Depository. I contacted the program directors and explained the services and resources provided at the clinic. I emphasized that many of our walk-in and out-reach clients needed quality food and nutrition guidance for their children.

We agreed to a plan that the clinic would act as a pantry for clients to receive food and nutritional counseling for their children on a weekend basis. The plan was enacted the first weekend of November, 1993. We advertised in all the local communities. The initial weekend had a small turnout but gradually grew from week to week. By February, we were giving food continuously from morning to night. Nutritional advice was available on request.

By 2002, the clinic had come a long way since its initiation six years ago. We had acquired a good sized volunteer network, offered resources and support within and outside the clinic, partnered with health and social service agencies and instituted a food and information distribution center.

I was heartened by the success of the clinic, commitment of my students and the involvement of the volunteers. In a short period of time, our commitment had helped reduce the poverty levels of many families and children.

CHAPTER 34

KIDS COUNT

The success of the clinic provided the motivation to research other national data banks to identify the needs of families and children living in poverty. I identified an organization named Voices for Illinois Children, powered by YWCA, an independent advocacy organization that champions strong public policies and investments for all children in the state. Voices was affiliated with Illinois KIDS COUNT…a nationwide network of state-level projects supported by the Casey Foundation. The annual Illinois KIDS COUNT report is widely regarded as the most thorough examination of children's lives in the state. It uses the best available data to monitor the education, social-emotional, economic, and physical well-being of Illinois children. [56]

I scheduled an orientation meeting for all the volunteers to discuss the use of KIDS COUNT data to identify trends that would impact the delivery of resources and services within the drop-in and out-reach programs. I explained that the data would help identify race/ethnic, poverty, unemployment income, temporary assistance for needy families (TANF), supplemental nutrition assistance and housing needs of children throughout the state, county, and the city. The data would help identify the number of volunteers, resources, services, reach-out locations, bilingual, and food distribution needs. The volunteers were very receptive and willing to assist where needed.

I informed the volunteers that the KIDS COUNT data is obtained from the US census reports. The data is categorized by age group, race/ethnicity, and family. Economic well-being indicators include nativity, employment and income, public assistance, housing, and poverty. Educational indicators include early childhood, school age, young adults, and test scores. Family and community indicators include environment, family structure, birth outcomes, health insurance, vital statistics, dental health, and other health. Behavioral indicators include child abuse and neglect, juvenile justice, out of home placements, public safety, other safety, and risky behavior.

Demographic indicators include child population by gender, age group, race, and ethnicity and family nativity. The comprehensive collection of data for each state has been compiled since 1948. Illinois data became available in 1992. Voices annual KIDS COUNT data reports examined the quality of life facing children and families throughout the state including youth development. The county-level and statewide statistics demonstrate trends, illustrate needs, and support policy proposals.

Because the KIDS Count data is so comprehensive and detailed, I chose total population, race/ethnicity, poverty, unemployment, income, temporary assistance for needy families (TANF) and food stamp (SNAP) as data which would benefit the clinic walk-in and reach-out programs. The significance and importance of data and statistics offered the clinic an opportunity to project its staffing and the needs of families and children in the food stamp/ SNAP state, county, and city. [57]

I chose Illinois and Chicago data comparisons between 1990 and 2013. I felt that a ten to thirteen-year analysis of data would give a good understanding of trends. I reported the data to the volunteers in the following format.

Population

Between 1990 to 2010 *Chicago's* white and black populations decreased and the Asian population increased. The population trends suggest that resources and support for poor whites and blacks may decrease, and Asian needs may increase. [58]

Race/Ethnicity

Between 1990 and 2010 the *Chicago* County Asian/Latino race/ethnicity populations increased. The data suggest an increase in the poverty needs of Asians and Latino's

Poverty

In 1999, the poverty rate in Illinois was 14.3 and 21.0 in 2013...an increase of 6.7 percent. Chicago's poverty rate in 1999 was 28.5 and 35.0 in 2013... an increase of 6.5 percent. The data signals a need for targeted investments and policies across the state for all race/ethnicity groups.

Unemployment

Between 2010 and 2013 the unemployment rates for Chicago decreased from 10.6 percent to 9.3 percent respectively. The median income for all families with children from 1989 to 2010 increased. The data reveal that the incomes for all families with children was significantly higher than single father and mother incomes. The lowest incomes were reported for single fathers and mothers. Both groups represent the greatest number of clients seen at the clinic.

Temporary Assistance

Between 2009 and 2013 the average monthly temporary assistance for needy families *(TANF)* for *Illinois* increased. The data indicate a significant increase in monthly income assistance during a four-year period.

Between 2009 and 2013 the age of children receiving supplemental nutrition assistance (SNAP/food stamps) benefits in Illinois under five years was increased to seventeen years. The data suggest that the need for food stamps had increased in all age groups between 2009 and 2013.

Households

Between 2009 and 2013 the number of children living in *Illinois* households with high cost burden had decreased. The decrease may be correlated with a decrease in white and black populations. [59]

When the orientation was finished, a number of volunteers asked questions related to the data and gave recommendations as to how they could use the data to improve the walk-in and out-reach programs. I was pleased with the outcome of the orientation. We began using the trend data and suggestions the following day.

CHAPTER 35

PRESIDENTS AND POVERTY

I hadn't paid much attention to US presidential politics since John F. Kennedy (JFK) was elected in 1960. I was ten years old, and my life focus was not politics. I enjoyed the traditional boy stuff...sports, movies, and ice cream. My attention was drawn to politics when JFK was assassinated in 1963. He and his wife had become national and international celebrities, because of their youthfulness, athletic appearance and two beautiful children. I had no awareness of his political opinions or philosophies.

In 1963, I was thirteen years old and in the eighth grade. After JFK'S assassination, I had a slight interest in politics. I had heard and read about the plight of the black people and the racism and discrimination that existed in America, especially the South. I also developed a concern for families and children in poverty. I had no exposure to the poor, either white or black. At the time, I had no hint that poverty would become my life's work.

Upon John Kennedy's death, Lyndon B. Johnson (LBJ) assumed the remainder of Kennedy's four-year term and was elected an additional four year (1963 to 1969). LBJ accomplished a number of political wins. He passed a major tax cut, the Clean Air Act and the Civil Rights Act of 1964. Additionally, he passed the Social Security Amendment of 1965 and created two government-run healthcare programs, Medicare, and Medicaid. [60]

I followed LBJ's sweeping reforms through my high school years and continued to develop an interest in presidents who proposed policies and legislation that helped poor families and children.

In 1969, Richard Nixon was elected as the 37th president. His term was plagued with controversy and scandal. Despite the negatives, Nixon did establish diplomacy with China, a slow ending of the Vietnam War and environmental protection standards.

He created the Office of Economic Opportunity (OEO) which administered most of the war on poverty programs created by Lyndon Johnson. The OEO was responsible for creating the Job Corps, Volunteers in Service to America (VISTA), head start and (CETA) Comprehensive Employment and Training Act. The program provided training for low-income persons.

Nixon was also responsible for reforming the Department of Health Education and Welfare, Child Food Assistance Program, expansion of the Food Stamp Program, FAP, Council for Urban Affairs and the Housing and Community Development Act. [61]

By restructuring the OEO and enacting the Revenue-Sharing Act of 1962, Nixon took "steps toward combating the bureaucratic inactivity that too often undermined the antipoverty offensive." He achieved some of what he promised on the antipoverty front.

Nixon's ambitious domestic agenda went a long way toward ending hunger in the US. Congress passed and signed the welfare reform proposals. He increased federal assistance for the poor by shifting programs to direct financial aid and spent a lot on social welfare. [62]

He was often criticized about his commitment to welfare reform, national health insurance and the cities. His moral and legal transgressions (Watergate Scandal) prevented him from achieving his domestic goals.

During Nixon's presidency, I worked as a janitor at DuShane High School, and attended City College, working toward an associate degree in Human Services. I continued to follow the progress of presidents to combat poverty. I had become cognizant of the numerous programs that three presidents had fostered (JFK, LBJ, RMN). All of whom had been successful to some degree. However, families and children continued their battles with nutrition/food, housing, education and employment.

In 1974, Gerald R. Ford became the 38th president. He assumed the presidency after Nixon's resignation. Domestically, Ford presided over the worst economy in four decades. However, he cut inflation, decreased unemployment, and cut the growth of crime.

He carried out food stamp reform, improved the effectiveness of Aid to Families with Dependent Children (AFDC) welfare programs, reduced unemployment from 8.9 percent to 7.7 percent and replaced housing categorical grants with state block grants. Although Ford's efforts to influence poverty weren't noteworthy, he was considered trustworthy and presented a strong moral image.

"Ford never offered a grand vision or a viable program to alleviate the misery of those at the bottom of the faltering economy. So, Congress kept on spending, Ford kept on vetoing, and too many poor people kept on suffering." [63]

While Ford was in office, I had completed high school and moved from the South Side projects. My experience going to an all-black school and living in the projects had strengthened my desire and passion to work with poor families and children.

I was twenty-seven years old when Jimmy Carter became the 39th president of the US. He served a one-year term from 1977 to 1981. I had completed my Bachelor of Science degree and was working as a counselor for SSSD. I had become totally immersed in the needs of families and children in poverty. Carter's presidency couldn't have been more important to me.

Carter's accomplishments included finding peaceful solutions to international conflicts, advancing democracy and human rights and promoting social development. In 1979, Carter submitted a welfare reform message to congress in two bills: the Social Welfare Reform Amendments and the Work Training Opportunities Act. These proposals would address the key failings of the welfare system, promote efficiency, improve incentives and opportunities to work, and substantially improve the incomes of millions of poor people. A major part of Carter's proposal was the improvement for the Aid to Families with Dependent Children (AFDC) and food stamp programs. The changes targeted needy individuals who are eligible but do not participate in the food stamp program and simplified the welfare system. Carter's proposals to overhaul welfare programs were rejected by Congress because they increased government spending. Carter's attempt to help families and children in poverty failed, but he left a caring legacy and a plan for future presidents. [64]

During the Carter campaign, I had worked as a volunteer. I believed in his ideas to help the poor. I spent an inordinate amount of time and energy to help get him elected and was elated when he won. I was disappointed that he did not win a second term, but his efforts captured my attention and motivated me to continue my pursuit to help people in poverty.

In 1981, Ronald Reagan became the 40th president of the US. He believed that social programs would not stimulate the economy and lift Americans out of poverty. Reagan believed that lowering taxes and cutting social welfare programs would create a strong economy with many jobs.

Reagan cut Aid to Families with Dependent Children (AFDC) spending and allowed states to require welfare recipients to participate in workfare programs. He believed that social programs would not stimulate the economy and lift Americans out of poverty. Reagan believed that lowering taxes and cutting social welfare programs would create a strong economy and create jobs.

Reagan's economic policies during his two terms (1981 to 1989) crippled the poor. The rate of poverty at the end of his two terms was the same as in 1980. Cutbacks during the Reagan years helped increase both poverty and inequality. [65]

In 1989, George H.W. Bush became the US 41st president and a one term president. His major accomplishments that affected the lives of families and children in poverty included the Americans with Disabilities Act (1990) and the Civil Rights Act of (1991). The legislation made it easier to sue employers on the grounds of discrimination, raised the minimum hourly wage and provided a $1.3 trillion tax cut.

The American Disability Act became law in 1990. The civil rights legislation prohibited individuals in all areas of public life, including jobs, schools, transportation and all public and private places that are open to the general public.

Bush was unwilling to fulfill the administration's anti-poverty objectives, and the plight of the poor worsened under his watch. The poverty rate rose from 13 percent to almost 15 percent. When Bush left office there were more than seven million more Americans below the poverty line than when he entered. It has been said that if Bush were able to rally twenty-eight nations to fight aggression abroad just imagine if he had rallied his own nation to fight poverty at home. [66]

In 1993, William J. Clinton (Bill) became the 42nd US president. His accomplishments included the creation of 22 million jobs, the lowest employment rate in 30 years, raised educational standards, increased school choice, doubled education and training investment, lowered welfare rolls to the lowest numbers in 32 years and raised higher incomes at all levels. African American yearly incomes increased by nearly $7,000 in 1993, all income brackets experienced double-digit growth, the bottom 20 percent saw the largest income growth at 16.3 percent, and lowest poverty rate in 20 years… his economic plan included paying off a $360 billion debt.

President Clinton's domestic accomplishments were praised by many Americans, especially black Americans. His policies and programs reduced poverty rates and raised income levels. The Clinton presidency's economic impact on African Americans in the south reduced unemployment from 14.2 percent in 1992 to 8.9 percent in 1998, raised the median income of African American households from 4.3 percent in 1997 to 15 percent between 1993 and 97 and real wages rose 5.2 for men and 6.2 for women.

Additionally, his presidency saw the largest drop in African American poverty in more than twenty-five years from 33.1 to 26.5 percent, child poverty dropped to the lowest level on record 39.9 to 37.2 percent and minimum wage increases benefited 1. 3 million African Americans. His plethora of policies influenced an increase in small business loans, housing vouchers, home ownership and fair housing. His initiatives contributed significantly to reducing housing problems throughout the US. He extended the family leave act, eliminated racial and ethnic health disparities, extended health care to millions of children (CHIP), increased Women, Infant and Children (WIC) funding and made the largest investment in education in 30 years. [67]

Needless to say, I was a strong admirer of Clinton's programs and policies. My research on presidents from 1960 to 2001 revealed that he had a greater impact on African Americans than any previous president. His employment, income, housing, health, and education initiatives reduced poverty and provided valued assistance for families and children.

In 2001, George W. Bush, President George H. W. Bush's son, was elected as the 43rd president of the US. He served two terms from 2001 to 2009. Accomplishments that had an impact on families and children in poverty included a $1 trillion tax cut, an education reform bill known as No Child Left Behind (NCLB), overhauled Medicare, and a $145 billion stimulus package in response to a housing crisis and rapidly increasing oil prices.

The tax cuts put more money in the hands of consumers and NCLB acted as an anti-poverty program because it was based on an implicit assumption that increased educational achievement was the route out of poverty for low-income families and individuals. [68]

NCLB had its pros and cons. The overall goal was to provide students in disadvantaged areas an equal opportunity to learn compared to other students in the US. It never really addressed the core issues behind poor student learning. Factors such as large classroom size, poor building conditions or student hunger were not addressed. One of its premises was that teachers and administrators paid little attention to the students with the poorest grades. The idea was that the best students would pass and the students with the worst grades would never make it anyway.

I had become familiar with the educational needs of poor children when I attended DuSable High School for two years, and when I worked as a teacher's aide in an alternative school for four years. During that six-year period, I observed many poor students who struggled academically. NCLB had become the educational law of the land. I believe it did more harm than good for poor families and children.

I had developed a theory that disadvantaged children could learn better in classrooms with fewer students, a more modified yet rigorous curriculum, teachers who knew not only what to teach (content) but how (pedagogical content knowledge) to teach to the individual needs of each child. I believed that many students don't learn the first time and that after school or at the beginning of school academic tutorials should be available for all students. What's wrong with not getting it until the second or third try?

Barack Obama became the 44th president of the United States in 2009 and served two terms. His accomplishments to help the poor included The Child Care and Development block grant of 2014. It provided grants to states so they could assist low-income families in finding childcare for their children. The American Recovery and Reinvestment Act of 2009 saved and created jobs and provided relief to those most affected by the economic crisis of 2008-2009. Additional policies included school grants for underperforming schools. The Affordable Care Act of 2010 (ACA) (Obamacare) provided affordable health insurance for all Americans, offered patient protection and became the most significant regulatory makeover of the US healthcare since the 1960s. The ACA's major provisions came in 2014. By 2016, the law increased quality, affordability and access to healthcare. The Healthy Hunger-Free Kids Act of 2010 funded nutrition and free lunch programs, set new standards for schools and allocated money for the implementation of these provisions. [69]

Barack Obama's poverty policies and programs impacted millions of poor families and children in all states and especially in impoverished cities. The Affordable Care Act (ACA) benefitted millions of Americans especially people who were unemployed or had low paying jobs. More than 20 million Americans obtained health insurance coverage within the first five years of the ACA. Other provisions of the Act included more affordable health insurance, coverage for people with preexisting conditions, no time limits exit on care, more screenings were covered, prescriptions, and drug costs were reduced. [70]

The effect of the ACA on poor families and children who don't have health insurance and those who buy insurance on the individual market was mixed. It helped those who have no insurance because they cannot afford it or because they have conditions which made the premiums too high. Those individuals who benefited the least from ACA were the poor and uninsured who live in states that did not choose to expand Medicaid. If you were one of the twenty states that did not expand Medicaid you can buy coverage, but you are not eligible for subsidies. Millions of poor families and children who live in states that did not expand Medicare were left without insurance coverage and the benefit of other provisions in the Act. Despite the Act's attempt to provide affordable health care for all, it fell short of helping millions of families and children in poverty. [71]

Conclusion

My research and review of ten president's beliefs and legislative policies on poverty from 1960 to 2017 is frustrating and confusing. It seems that each president empathized with the plight of the poor but was often thwarted in their efforts to help. Presidents were influenced by their own belief system or other factors like Congressional partisanship, term length, political party affiliation, American voter apathy, foreign wars, poor economy, world events, poor advisement, power/control, ego, mental/physical health, constituents, lobbyists, wealthy contributors, reelection, racism, discrimination, bigotry, despotism, nepotism, filibuster, majority, super majority, compensation, or benefits. The list goes on and on. Whether it was any one president or his beliefs or one or more of the numerous factors that contribute to making the right decision for poor families and children are not relevant. The point is that poor Americans and especially African Americans have not benefited from the reforms, Acts, laws, etc. have been promised or legislated for hundreds of years. It seems that the positives of one presidency become the negatives of another. What's wrong with giving legislation a chance to succeed before it is ousted by a change in presidents, political party or by a majority change in the Senate or House of Representatives? The American people, and especially the poor, are victims of a political system that needs to be changed.

My exposure to poverty, although situational, illustrates that generational poverty has negatively influenced family health, housing, education, work and life expectancy. A child living in poverty for generations affects their emotional, cognitive, and behavioral development, education and social and health outcomes that cause adolescent problems, academic failure, antisocial behavior, drug abuse, depression, sexual abuse, an increase in school dropout numbers and low graduation rates.

Poor African Americans continue to live in poverty. They are stuck in segregated neighborhoods, unemployed, underemployed, and working in minimum wage jobs. They often work long hours, have no health coverage, and need skill training to advance. The poor housing situations compound their struggle because of evictions, foreclosures and building repair needs.

Two nondiscriminatory terms that have surfaced recently are "equity" and "equality." Equity refers to the quality or ideal of being just, impartial, and fair. It is a structural and systemic concept that involves trying to understand and give people what they need to enjoy a full and healthy life. Equality aims to ensure that everyone gets the same things in order to enjoy life. If the US government were to ensure that all Americans have the opportunity to achieve equityand equality, our democracy would flourish.

CHAPTER 36
RETIREMENT

As my 65th birthday approached, I began to think that it was time to retire from my clinic directorship and teaching position at the University of Chicago. I had worked at UC for fourteen years and felt I had made a positive impact on poverty in the south side area of Chicago where I had lived all of my life (1950 to 2015). My forewarned and recent heart attack added encouragement to retire.

The clinic had progressed well...the walk in and out-reach programs were extremely successful. On the average, the clinic would see more than ten families per day whose needs were varied. Single mothers with a limited income would request information about state and federal programs. Teen mothers would request information about nutrition recommendations and help for their newborns. Single fathers would inquire about child care assistance and resources. Our volunteers were well armed with data, resources, and moral support and available informed and ready to help with all needs.

The research courses I taught offered students an opportunity to realize the importance of data to make informed decisions about the poverty needs of families and children in Illinois and the Chicago areas. Their commitment to volunteer at the clinic was unmeasurably overwhelming. I was proud of the university, local agency and community volunteers who spent countless hours at the clinic and in the outreach community locations helping the poor.

Recognizing that my efforts were on track and moving forward, I decided to retire. I talked to Latisha about my decision, and she was fully supportive. She asked, "What will you do to occupy your time?" I said, "I plan on volunteering at the clinic and the food deposition center and also, have given some thought to researching and writing about poverty. I would like to spend more time with our four grandchildren." Latisha responded, "I think you got it covered."

The following day, I made an appointment with the dean to talk about my pending retirement. I was surprised when his secretary forwarded my phone call to him within seconds. I hadn't mentioned why I wanted to meet with the dean. Maybe he was anticipating my call. The dean answered my call with, "What's up Louis?" I responded, "Thanks for taking my call so quickly." He said, "I thought it might be important, and I have heard rumors about you retiring." "Yes, I have decided to retire at the end of the semester which ends in two weeks." He said, "we will miss you but support your decision… you have made an indelible mark on our university and community. Your efforts to help poor families and children in our community is unmatched." Let's get together and plan your departure celebration." I said, "Thanks for your comments and all the support and resources you have given me over the years." Our discussion ended and I gathered my personal items and walked out of the door that I had known as "home" for fourteen years.

I received a call from the dean's office a couple of days later asking when I would be available for a retirement party. I was surprised that the office called and said, "There was no need for the celebration." The dean's secretary said, "Yes, there is…when are you available?" I said, "Choose a date, and I will be there reluctantly. She said, "Okay, I will let you know the date." Without my knowledge, the date was already chosen…December 28th at seven o'clock at the University assembly hall.

Latisha and I arrived at the UC ten minutes late and were greeted by my brother Peter and his family, Mindy and her family and Rosie. When we walked into the assembly hall, I was shocked at the number of people seated.

They all rose and clapped loudly…I was humbled and speechless. As we walked toward the stage, I recognized many of the faculty, students, friends and, more importantly, many of the community residents who benefited from the clinic resources and services. I nodded to each person and thanked them for their greeting and attendance. When we arrived at the front of the assembly hall, Latisha and I were welcomed by the university president and the dean of the psychology program. We were seated at the front table and our family claimed seats in the front row. The university president approached the podium and began his introduction mentioning my list of personal and clinic accomplishments. I was humbled and gratified. Within minutes, I was standing before more than a hundred people. I had written some words to thank everyone but decided to speak off the cuff. I thanked all for coming and began telling a story.

> "Once upon a time, there was a young boy who grew up similar to many others on the south side of Chicago. He attended a local pubic elementary school with neighborhood friends and enjoyed The customary activities of the day… sports, goofing off, picking on each other and more.
>
> When he reached junior high, he continued his boyhood friendships but added an interest in the opposite sex. School was very important to him, as was a desire to help others.
>
> When he started high school, his life stayed the course until his father died suddenly. Without his financial support his mother, brother and two sisters had to move to a different section of the South Side. His life changed drastically. He was forced to live and go to school in an area of distressed poverty.
>
> He accepted the changes and began to realize that his new living situation would influence his future work. After six

> years, he had realized his desire to help the poor and that brings me to today.
>
> Without that poverty exposure, I would not be standing in front of you. My career goals would not have been achieved without the support of my mother, brother, and sisters, friends and colleagues. The true heroes of day are the volunteers who gave so freely their time and energy the past sixteen years. Last but more importantly, I would like to give credit to the thousands of families who took advantage of all the resources and services that the clinic offered to them.
>
> Thank you all from the bottom of my heart. I may be retiring from the university but not the clinic. See you around."

The crowd rose and expressed their adulation with cheers, whistles, and thundering claps. I was overwhelmed as I struggled back to my seat. Latisha greeted me with a hug, kiss, and a Kleenex.

The dean walked to the podium and asked me to stand by his side. I was certainly in no condition to do so, but somehow managed to reach him. He opened a purple velvet box and held up a blue ribbon with a gold medal attached. He began, "It is the university's pleasure, the volunteers' desire and the communities' will that I present you with the University of Chicago's Humanitarian award." The audience stood and cheered.

The crowd broke up and moved toward the dining area. I was surrounded by my mother, brother and sisters, grandchildren, friends, colleagues, and families from the community. It was a special day that I would recall repeatedly.

The following week, I met with the food depository director and put together a weekly volunteer schedule. We agreed that I would work three days a week for four hours. I started the next day. It was a different role for me, one that I adjusted to quickly. The day went by quickly without a hitch. I must have boxed over a hundred canned goods. I got home and Latisha greeted me at the door. "How did your first day as a volunteer go?" she asked. "Fine, the day went by quickly," I said. "I especially like working just four hours." I continued working at the depository and eventually grew into my volunteer role.

I decided that I had a couple more hours in a day to fill, so I volunteered at the clinic two days a week for four hours. I was very familiar with the responsibilities and soon grew accustomed to my new role. The most difficult part was getting others to realize I was no longer their boss...I was one of them.

Latisha and I gradually became more acquainted with our four grandchildren. We would take day trips with them to parks and lakes and occasionally a vacation to the ocean beaches. We enjoyed our time with them, and I found that I did not miss the daily routine of managing the clinic and teaching.

Occasionally, I would receive a request as a guest speaker. Area high schools and community groups would call for a "rags to riches" speech about my life to inspire students and motivate teens. I frequently did not accept the invitation. I felt that my story was not unique and that there were many other speakers with better and more words to part with.

I continued to possess an interest in politics. Donald J. Trump had been elected the 45th US president following Barack Obama. I was interested in seeing how a "businessman" would run the country. His presidency began on January 20, 2016, and because I had the time and interest in his policies for the poor, I followed his every move.

CHAPTER 37
DONALD J. TRUMP

Trump became the 45th US president and took office on January 20, 2017. He was left with economic legacy of following America's first black president. Within six months of his presidency, he claimed that he had strengthened the economy since Obama left office. I decided to research his claim and identified an article written by NBC's Dante Chinni on August 23, 2020. The article was titled, "What Did Trump Inherit from Obama?" Chinni offered data to refute Trump's claim that he built a great economy. The data proved that he inherited it from Obama.

Chinni reported that the average quarterly economic growth under Trump was 25 percent. The percentage compared exactly with Obama's in his second term. Additionally, Obama left Trump had an unemployment rate of 4.7 percent, a decrease of 3.12 percent from when he took office. Obama's 2015 income data results were 2 percent higher than the year before he took office. Also, more people we're working, and stock prices soared. In 2015, because of Obama's policies, millions of Americans had incomes that had risen above the poverty line. [72]

The 2016 presidential election between Hillary Clinton and Donald Trump was controversial in many ways. The democratic candidate, Hillary Rodham Clinton, was the wife of former president Bill Clinton. That in itself presented a huge challenge for the Republicans. Bill Clinton left the White House after two terms with a thriving economy and no federal deficit. His presidency was envied by most Republicans. To take back the presidency in

2016 was a goal that led to Donald Trump's nomination. Many Republican party members and voters believed that a "businessman" would "Make America Great Again." A slogan that Trump adopted while campaigning and during his presidency.

The Democratic presidential candidate for president was Hillary Clinton. She had a tough road ahead of her after winning the Democratic nomination. The at-large media and Democratic voters viewed her personality as a negative. She was considered harsh, strongly opinionated and too forthright. She was disliked by Republicans, although some thought she was the ideal candidate for Trump to beat. The general public view depicted her as a person who was not trustworthy. Trump capitalized on the view and gave her the name "Crooked Hillary." Trump, Republicans and some Democrats were critical of her links to Wall Street, using a private email server for official public communications rather than official State Department accounts and security failures that contributed to the attack on the Benghazi consulate when she was Obama's Secretary of State. [73]

I felt that the negative attention that Hillary Clinton garnered as the wife of the Arkansas Governor and US president might be attributed to her independence, liberal perspective and feminist attitude. She was extremely outspoken and frequently acquired enemies in and outside politics.

The outcome of the 2016 presidential election between Clinton and Trump was surprising. The polls and media had Clinton winning the popular vote and the electoral college. The results of the election showed that Trump lost the popular vote by more than 2.8 million votes but won 30 states and the electoral college with 304 electoral votes to Clinton's 227. The tumultuous and abrasive 2016 election defied established political norms. Almost every poll pointed to a comfortable victory for Clinton, but Trump's anti-Washington appeal to white working-class voters overcame Clinton's predicted victory. [74]

The reasons why Hillary Clinton lost the electoral college vote were credited to Trump's ability to galvanize white voters without college degrees, particularly in the Rust Belt. She lost African American and millennial voters who were not inspired by her candidacy. Her message to working-class voters was weak. She talked about taxing the rich, redistributing wealth and creating new benefits. She rarely talked about jobs that would have resonated with the working class of all races.

Donald Trump began his four-year term concentrating on unemployment, household incomes, and poverty. Much of the published data was often questionable...US census reports were inaccurate because of "statistical flukes," new data processing procedures, data adjustment factors, ambiguous survey questions, inflation adjustments and COVID-19 all clouded data results.

Unemployment

Trump's unemployment percentage was 3.5. percent during his first year in office. The lowest percentage in a half century. However, in January 2020, job growth slowed then collapsed as COVID-19 led to mass unemployment. Unemployment increased after nine years. The longest streak on record. More than 22 million jobs disappeared.

Household Incomes

During the first two years of Trump's presidency household incomes soared. In 2016, there was a 3.1 percent increase and in 2017 a 1.8 percent increase. In 2018, the US Census Bureau's measure of median household income reached $63,179, an increase of $1,400 from 2016. As income rose, the rate of poverty declined. In 2017, Americans living with incomes below the official poverty line went down to 12.3 percent of the population.

Poverty Rate

The rate of poverty declined for three consecutive years. The December 2018 census reported that close to 1 million fewer people were in poverty in 2017 compared with 2016. In 2018, the poverty level decreased from 3.5 to 2.5 million.

In 2019, the US Census Bureau reported that 5.1 million fewer people were in poverty...a reduction of 1.6 percentage points. Poverty declined three consecutive years dropping by 1.3 percentage points. The percentage of Americans living below the poverty line decreased from 6.6 2.2 percent.

When Trump took office the poverty rate in the US was around 18 percent. In January 2020 the poverty rate rose considerably due to the unprecedented health crisis. More than one in ten Americans suffered from food insecurity and 87 million resorted to food stamps. The impact of COVID-19 on poverty did not impact all Americans equally. Poor families without jobs, health insurance and access to resources and support were affected significantly.

In 2020, as COVID-19 spiraled across the country and especially in poor communities many states witnessed the largest increase in US poverty ever recorded. The poverty rate surged from 9.3 percent in June to 11.7 percent in November. It was the largest increase since 1960. [75]

African Americans and Hispanics were disproportionately affected. One of six Americans suffered from food insecurity including 18 million children. The US was without a doubt poorer at the end of the Trump presidency. "The president deprived the country of crucial weapons in the fight against poverty."

In 2020, it was projected that the poverty rate for whites would be 9.2 percent, non-Hispanic 6.6 percent and black non-Hispanic 15.2 percent because of Covid 19. [76]

A significant departure from the policies of President Obama was President Trump's attempt to thwart Obamacare. The very day that Trump took office, January 20, 2017, he signed an executive order instructing administrative officials "to wave, defer, grant exemptions from, or delay" implementing parts of the Affordable Care Act. Congress readied itself to repeal and replace Obama's signature law. The repeal and replace and the approach to piecemeal ACA failed. There were some changes to the law during Trump's term, but the law is still in effect and continued attempts to repeal it were negated on June 21, 2021, when the Supreme Court threw out the ACA lawsuit, not the ACA. [77]

Conclusions

President Obama left office after eight years on a positive note. His energy and positive attitude was infectious. Millions of Americans had grown to like and respect his domestic accomplishments. His policies influenced a decrease in unemployment and poverty and an increase in household income.

The media and millions of Democrats, Republicans and independents believed that Trump's one year term was marred with a personality of abrasiveness, lies, arrogance and a negative moral compass. Despite his lack of appeal by many, millions of Americans supported his policies and overlooked his personality and attitude.

Obama's domestic policies resulted in a decrease in unemployment and poverty and an increase in household income. However, the effects of the pandemic erased his domestic accomplishments. Poverty rates increased almost 2.0 percentage points because of COVID-19. There is a school of thought expressed by millions that if Trump had been reelected his policies would have continued to lower unemployment and poverty and increase incomes.

The possibility of Trump continuing his economic gains were dashed because of his unpopularity with blacks, females, suburban residents, and college educated voters. His loss to Joe Biden was convincing in the popular vote outcome and in the final electoral count.

CHAPTER 38

COVID - 19

The following is a real-time poverty report that estimated the effects of the COVID-19 pandemic from January through November 2020 and that was published in July 2021, by Zhejiang University, University of Chicago, NBER, AEI and the University of Notre Dame. [78]

The report used data from the US Census Bureau on real-time poverty that was published on December 15, 2020, and became public in July 2021. It emphasized that poverty continued to rise as the Coronavirus increased. The report stressed that the pandemic took a significant toll on the US labor market. Since the start of the pandemic, more than 86 million claims for unemployment insurance had been filed. More than 10.7 million individuals are unemployed, and millions of others are without jobs. [79]

A question is posed in the report: "What will be the long-term impact of the pandemic on individuals and families living in poverty?" Initially, poverty declined in the first few months of the pandemic. The poverty rate fell by 1.5 percentage points from 10.9 to 9.4. Poverty also declined for people with low levels of education and for those who fall into the "other race" (neither white nor black) category. The recent overall rise raises concerns about possible future increases in poverty from the pandemic.

From January through June poverty declined across a range of demographic groups and geographies. Since then, poverty has risen sharply. It rose by 2.4 percentage points from 9.3 per cent to 11.7 percent from June to November, adding 7.8 million to the poverty number. Despite the early decline during the pandemic, as of June 2020 poverty was higher than January 2020.

The entire decline in poverty through June can be accounted for by the one-time stimulus checks issued in April and May. Also, the expansion and increase of unemployment insurance and benefits. Without the $1,200 payment to individuals and the $2,400 payment to married couples with dependents, poverty would have risen sharply.

The increase of poverty in recent months was higher for blacks, children, and those with a high school education or less. For blacks, poverty had risen by 3.1 percentage points since June. The poverty rates by race from January through November 2020 for whites increased from 9.4 percent to 10.1 percent, an increase of 70 percent,; for blacks the rate increased from 18.2 percent to 21.3 percent, an increase of 3.10 percent; the "other" category decreased from 12.4 percent to 12.1 percent a decrease of 0.3 percent. The data indicate that the pandemic adversely affected blacks more than whites and individuals in the "other" category. [80]

The coronavirus pandemic was first reported late in 2019. The first case in the US was detected in February 2020. Its legitimacy, severity, and impact on Americans was questioned by President Trump, Republicans, health officials and the American people.

President Trump's initial cavalier attitude toward the coronavirus set a frightening example. He held fundraisers without social distancing or masks. 'It's a hoax. There's no pandemic,' said Trump on October 3, 2020. By July 25, 2020, the US recorded 154,000 coronavirus deaths and 1.87 million new cases. Despite the alarming numbers, Trump equated the virus to the flu while hospitalized for contracting it. He rarely mentioned the increasing numbers and death rates and ignored its effects entirely. The media and millions of Americans felt his leadership at a time of worldwide trauma and peril was despicable. Despite his beliefs, millions of Americans followed his lead and ignored the repeated warnings and guidelines offered by health officials in the US. [81]

COVID – 19 had a significant impact on me. It was one of the contributors that inspired me to write my story about poverty.

CHAPTER 39

JOE BIDEN

Joe Biden's victory over President Trump was disputed by millions of American voters, Congress, state and local politicians and the conservative media. President Trump called the results a "lie" and encouraged some states to challenge the popular vote and the electoral college results with recounts. A few states including Arizona, Georgia, Texas, and Pennsylvania had recounts but found no inequities to change the election results. Trump and his supporters were outraged, and challenges were made in the courts. The lawsuits did not change the election outcome. Millions of Americans who supported Trump argued that the election was stolen and Democrats in Congress were responsible. The outcome...the attempted takeover of the Capital building on January 6, 2021. [82]

President Biden took office on January 20 with the results of the election still viewed as questionable by millions of Trump supporters. Despite the controversy, Biden offered a lengthy agenda for his first 100 days in office. His plan dealt with reversing the corporate tax, enacting climate change legislation, extending the voting rights act, making comprehensive immigration changes, reforming the police and criminal justice systems, repairing global alliances, strengthening the economy and enacting education reforms. [83]

Biden took office during a time of crisis...with the coronavirus gripping the world. During his first 100 days, he signed a host of executive orders related to the pandemic and pushed a $1.9 trillion relief bill. His promise to fulfill one of his key campaign promises concerning the fight against the virus was achieved. AP reports that he has fulfilled 25 out of 61 promises and has started on 33 others. [84]

One of the most important promises Biden made was to build on the existing American Care Act enacted by President Obama while Biden was Vice-president. Despite Trump's vow to repeal and replace Obamacare, on June 17, 2021 the US Supreme Court upheld Obamacare in a 7 to 2 ruling, preserving the landmark law and its key protections for millions of people with preexisting conditions. The law continued to expand Medicaid for poor Americans and made private health plans more affordable for lower-income families. [85]

The Supreme Court ruling was crucial in helping families and children in poverty, especially blacks and Hispanics. The disparity between equitable and equal rages on. The poor with limited incomes, unemployment, and lack of healthcare continue to suffer. Housing, nutrition, food and a path toward reducing poverty continues to demonstrate unfairness between the haves and the have-nots.

One of President Biden's most pressing issues was COVID-19. To combat the pandemic, he assembled a task force to manage the surge; report infections; ensure the vaccines were safe, efficiently, and free of cost; and that at-risk populations were protected. The new coronavirus aid package included coordination with state governors, mayors, and local politicians. It expanded testing resources, increased the capacity to make personal protective equipment (PPE) and dealt with COVID racial and ethnic disparities.

Plans and Proposals

President Biden had proposed a number of initiatives to help the economy, healthcare, infrastructure, and jobs. His physical infrastructure plan includes 1.2 trillion dollars for building and rebuilding roads and bridges, broadband expansion to rural areas, and the construction of lead-free pipes for drinking water.

In addition to the physical infrastructure plan, Biden has proposed a human infrastructure plan of 3.5 trillion dollars that includes massive investments in the environment, housing, education and health care. His American Jobs Plan includes spending 2 trillion dollars in eight years on infrastructure to create millions of jobs, address climate change and raise the corporate tax rate. [85]

Biden's infrastructure proposals have stalled in the House of Representatives. His plans have been challenged by moderates and progressives. Moderates want to reduce the cost of the human infrastructure plan and the progressives want to maintain the proposed 3.5 trillion dollars. Theoutcome is uncertain.

Biden's Care Plan proposal protects Obamacare, gives Americans' more choice, reduces healthcare costs and make the system less complex, imposes tax credits, expands coverage to low-income Americans, lowers prescription drug costs and invests in community health centers. [86]

Conclusion

I believe that President Biden is on the right track. Jobs, health care, physical and human infrastructure and education are priorities that will help millions of families and children escape generational poverty. Additionally, his plans to tackle the effects of COVID-19 on the poor are underway.

The inequities and inequalities that exist between the poor and non-poor has reared its ugly head. For too long, president after president has enacted laws to combat poverty, but it still exists. My major concern centers on the reversal of poverty legislation either by executive order or by Congress. It only hurts the poor. Why can't something that is working be given a chance to help instead of being repealed by a change in presidency or political party? A good example is President Obama's Affordable Care Act. President Trump's first move was to terminate it instead of making changes to make it better for the poor. Don't get me wrong. I am not naïve. I am a pragmatist who believes in positive change for the good, regardless of personal agendas or unwarranted power or control. Let's Help the People!

CHAPTER 40

JANUARY 6, 2021

The attack on the US Capitol on January 6, 2021, by rioters supporting President Donald Trump's attempts to overturn his defeat in the 2020 presidential election against Joe Biden was the first attempt toward a "coup" in American history. Millions of Americans sat in front of their TVs in dismay. Is this really happening? Is an American president inciting a riot to overturn an election? Is this some third world country? Questions I posed to Latisha as we watched in horror.

Following the insurrection, President Trump and several Republican members of Congress addressed the crowd, repeating unfounded claims of electoral fraud. From Trump's outdoor podium, he encouraged his followers to "fight like hell" to "take back our country." He suggested that they march to the Capitol and promised he would be with them…he ran to a secure location. The demonstrators turned violent and breached police barricades, vandalized and ransacked parts of the building for hours. Five people died and more than 150 Capitol protectors were injured. [88]

It was the most tragic day of my life…nothing that I encountered during my lifetime could compare. I was in shock!

The entire conflict was "inspired by the lies" of President Trump, some Republican members of Congress and The Trump's white supremacist followers. A select commission was proposed to evaluate the riot so that the reasons for the insurrection could be determined and to assure that it would not happen again. The House Democrats were able to create a committee with two Republican representatives. The study is currently underway... the results to follow.

Although this tragic event had nothing to do with poverty; the action directly influenced the course of history and its effect on Democracy...the lifeline for the poor.

CHAPTER 41

EQUITY AND EQUALITY

My TIME magazine arrived just as I was about to write my final chapter. I decided that previous comments about equity and equality in the Presidents and Poverty chapter needed more attention.

As discussed, *Equity* refers to the quality or ideal of being just, impartial, and fair. It is a concept that involves trying to understand and give people what they need to enjoy a full and healthy life. *Equality* aims to ensure that everyone gets the same things in order to enjoy life.

The cover of the TIME magazine read" Visions of Equity" by Mahita Gajanan,Vol., 197. No's 19-20, 2021. The article title was "40 Ways Forward: Accountable Steps for a More Equitable America." The timing of the magazine and article couldn't have been more perfect. The opening paragraph read, "The events of the past year...a global health crisis, mass protests against police brutality, a surge in hate crimes...laid bare the vast inequalities that have persisted in the US for centuries." To address the inequities, TIME compiled a list of actionable steps that the US could take to usher in an era of true social, political, and economic equity. I scanned the forty articles to find those that are related to poverty. I selected the following articles to write about: Enact Universal Health Care, Reform the Thrifty Food Plan, Integrate Schools, Implement Universal Housing Voucher, Close the Digital Divide, Change Public School Funding, End Homelessness, and Create Universal PRE-K. [89]

Enact Universal Health Care, Ady Barkin, Activist

The article begins with emphasizing that tens of millions of people are without the health care they need. The author recommends that lower drug prices and a strengthening and expansion of Medicare would move America closer to health care justice. [90]

The pandemic brought to the world, and specifically to the US, the need to provide universal health care to the poor. Scores of poor Americans were adversely affected by COVID-19 in many ways. Millions of African Americans were faced with no health insurance, doctors, access to the internet, transportation, and money to get tested or to get a shot and fear that the vaccine would be harmful.

It is quite obvious that health is essential to a productive life. If you are poor and suffer from mental or physical health issues, can't work, don't' have appropriate housing and are food dependent, then the chances are good that a poverty situation could be alleviated if universal health care were available. Equity would exist and people would enjoy a full and healthy life. Likewise, equality would exist to ensure that everyone gets the same things in order to enjoy life·

Reform the Thrifty Food Plan by Parker L. Gilkesson

Another critical step toward equity for people of color who live in poverty is to reevaluate the 46-year-old Thrifty Food Plan (TFP) and increase the benefits of the Supplemental Nutrition Assistance Program (SNAP) to reflect the current economy and updated data on food prices. [91]

TFP outlines nutrient-dense foods and beverages, their amounts and associated costs that can be purchased on a limited budget to support a healthy diet through nutritious meals and snacks. SNAP benefits provide food-purchasing assistance for low-income and no-income people. It is updated each year based on the cost of the TFP. Both programs are currently being reevaluated and the reevaluation will be completed by December 2022.

The benefits of both programs for the poor are noteworthy. The importance of a nutritious diet and food-purchasing assistance offer an equitable opportunity for people in poverty.

Integrate Schools by Noliwe Rooks, Scholar of Race and Gender at Cornell University

How does school integration create a more equitable America? Segregated, unequal and underfunded schools and the education received influence racism and physical violence. The impacts are educational, but also psychological, emotional, spiritual, and physical. These emotions suggest to poor children that they are simply less important than others. Candidly put, racial segregation is unhealthy. [92]

The two years that I attended a segregated, unequal, and underfunded high school continues to affect me today. I witnessed hundreds of teens who lived in poverty, attended a school that needed continuous maintenance, lacked instructional resources and support staff and were taught by uncertified teachers. Students realized that their education was affected adversely and that conditions would not change, so acceptance was inevitable generation after generation.

Pay Workers Fair Wages, Alejandro de la Garza

During the late sixties the federal minimum wage averaged $1.35 per hour. The minimum wage in 2021 is $7.25. Congress is responsible for raising the rate but is reluctant because of opposition from powerful industry groups. The National Employment Law Project (NELP) advocates raising the salary floor to meet inflation increases and productivity growth. The NELP reports that if both factors had been tracked since the '60s the minimum would stand at $20 per hour. [93]

My mother was fortunate to work at a meat packing plant after my father died. Her hourly rate was $3 per hour. It seems low today but compared to $1.35 it was considered a good hourly rate. My first job as a janitor paid minimum wage. I worked a forty-hour week and took home fifty dollars a week. I had no family expenses and gave my mother half to pay for rent, utilities and food. We struggled at times but were able to save some money to leave the projects.

By comparison, most of the families were larger than ours and if two members of the family worked forty hours their take home pay was $100 per week. Because my mother and I worked, our take home pay per week was almost $300. Our family was fortunate, but hundreds of families who lived in the projects had no way out and were forced to live generation after generation in poverty.

Implement Universal Housing Vouchers, Wes Moore, CEO of Robin Hood

In 2021, the National Low Income Housing Coalition reported that the housing problem for the poor in America existed before the pandemic in the US. Millions of Americans spend more than 50 percent of their income on rent or mortgages according to the Urban Institute. Lower-income families have been hit the hardest by the pandemic. To support poor families the federal government has funded the Housing Choice Voucher Program in which families have part of their rent subsidized by a federal voucher paid directly to the landlord. In reality, many landlords discriminate against racial minorities and families with children. Landlords frequently refuse to accept vouchers or offer limited housing choices to families with vouchers. Another problem with the program is that funding is far outpaced by the need. [94]

During his 2020 campaign, President Biden proposed a universal housing voucher program, which would fully fund the program to meet the eligible population. Data supports that when low-income families receive housing vouchers, they are less likely to experience food insecurity, be separated from their children and experience domestic violence.

While living in the projects, my exposure to the housing voucher problem was nonexistent. I had no knowledge or contact with families who had vouchers or were discriminated against by landlords. My mother and I had incomes to pay our rent each month, so we were never in need of vouchers. I do recognize that there were many families who were evicted from their apartments, because they could not pay their rent. Based on my limited awareness, I would support universal housing vouchers for eligible families.

Close the Digital Divide, Paulina Cachero

The digital divide that separates Americans was felt significantly by low-income families when COVID – 19 spread across the US. Families were unable to access information about the virus and were unaware of where to get tested or vaccinated. Millions of Americans were already struggling because they lacked access to broadband services. The problem worsened when hundreds of thousands of children were unable to attend school or learn remotely. Most of the children were living in poverty and had no money to buy a computer. Months without in-school learning or at-home learning cost poor children grade level regression in reading and math…not to mention the social, psychological, and emotional impact that will be felt for years.

To close the digital divide accessibility, affordability and technology learning need to be addressed by government, local communities, schools, and other public and private sectors. An attempt to alleviate the problem is underway. The FCC launched efforts to map gaps in coverage and created a program to subsidize the cost of internet services and devices. Telecom giants have offered lower-cost broadband options to consumers with an economic need. And the Biden administration proposed spending $100 billion to invest in "future proof" broadband networks. If the efforts fully materialize, I believe the divide may be closed. There will always be millionsof poor people who won't take advantage of one or more of these options for various personal and economic reasons. [95]

If the technology existed when I attended high school, I am sure the digital divide would have existed. There were a number of students that came to class without basic tools...pens, pencils, paper, notebooks, etc. If the basics weren't available, a computer would have been unimaginable.

Change Public-School Funding, Katie Reily

School funding depends heavily on property taxes. School districts located in affluent communities across America are at a distinct advantage. High-income families choose to live in wealthy districts because their children will have access to the best schools, teachers, support services and resources. Low-income families do not have that luxury. Their children attend neighborhood schools in large cities that do not have a tax base that is comparable to high-income families. To remedy the situation, it is suggested that the federal government should increase funding to schools serving low-income children, and states should target aid to students with the most needs and districts with lower poverty wealth. [96]

In 1964, when I attended DuSable High School it was quite apparent that the school could benefit from more funding. The tax base was much lower than neighboring city schools. The building itself needed continuous repair. Tables and chairs were broken or unavailable. Books were shared by students and often falling apart. Administrators and teachers complained, but the answer was...we don't have the money. I thought later in my life about the situation and always felt bad about my goal to get out rather than do something about it.

Create Universal PRE-K, Lydia Kiesling, Author

Research and data on the advantages of early childhood education has been documented For decades. Educators, psychologists, and behaviorists have reported a plethora of information that supports early start, head start and pre-k education programs. Coinciding with early childhood education is the need for daycare. It has become one of the greatest expenses facing parents of young children in America today. Being unable to send children to preschool forces women out of the workforce and has a negative impact on Black, brown, and low-income children who have less access to high quality programs. [97]

The Biden administration has recognized the overwhelming importance of childcare and preschool and has called for a tax on the wealthy to extend the opportunity to all. A version of Biden's plan has shown that providing universal, quality care is a part of the fight for social, racial and economic justice.

This chapter was an afterthought and was not included in my first draft. It has become a signature piece of my novel. Each of the articles I have discussed and commented on center on poverty. Without universal health care, quality food and nutrition programs, fair wages, improved housing programs, increased technological opportunities, changes in school funding and greater access for early childhood education, the chances are low for achieving *Equity* - the quality or ideal of being just, impartial, and fair and give people what they need to enjoy a full/ healthy life and *Equality* - ensuring that everyone gets the same things in order to enjoy life.

"America is not like a blanket: one piece of unbroken cloth, the same color, the same texture the same size. America is more like a quilt: many patches, many pieces, many colors, many sizes, all woven and held together by a common thread."
Jessie Louis Jackson

The common thread is that we are Americans regardless of race, ethnicity, age or gender. AllAmericans deserve equity and equality.

CHAPTER 42

FAMILY AND FRIENDS RECAP - 2021

My love for my siblings, Peter, Mindy, and Rosie continued to strengthen as the years passed. Peter was sixty-three and had retired from his manager position with Radio Shack. He and his wife Patricia had moved to the suburbs of Chicago and had raised four successful children. They struggled at times with the daily responsibilities of raising children. I think Peter's exposure to our four years of poverty contributed to his resiliency and determination for success and for his family. As the years passed, I hadn't seen much of Peter and his family, but during my retirement I plan on spending more time with them.

I saw Mindy and her family frequently as the years passed. She was sixty and still working at Chicago Med. Her two children had gone to college and followed in their mother's footsteps. Sandy, Mindy's older daughter, had become a doctor and Francie was a dentist. Mindy's husband, Felix, had died a few years ago and had contributed much to his family's success.

Rosie had retired from teaching and had never married. She was fifty-eight. She often said, "My students are my children and my legacy." She was very close to me, and we shared much during our time together. We would frequently recall our early childhood and its influence on careers and personal development. She had become a strong independent woman who had made her mark in becoming an exceptional person and teacher.

Our two foster children Robert and Raul had successful careers. Robert had become a well-known chef in the Chicago area. He owned his own restaurant that featured Chicago's celebrated favorites...pizza, beef sandwiches and hot dogs. Raul continued to work in the construction field and was successful in the real estate market. Both had struggles during the years. Robert was divorced from his partner Jim but had an amicable relationship as they raised their two adopted children. Raul never married but maintained an active social life with a troupe of women. Latisha and I were proud of the boys and often commented that they made our lives complete and worthwhile.

My lifelong friends who contributed so much to my career and my personal growth were always there for me over the years. Floyd, my mentor, and confidant for more than sixty years had died from COVID-19 last year. He fought the good fight but was unable to win the battle with the persistent virus. I attended his funeral and remained in contact with his wife and children. More than any other friendship this was one that was never ending.

Other friendships that had become important to me included Sheila from the alternative program and June from CCCS. Both continued to act as my friends and professional consultants. Their advice and encouragement made my career rewarding and my personal beliefs stronger.

I would be remiss if I didn't mention Latisha. She has been my sword and my shield for more than forty-five years. She was there when I needed a poke for motivation and a pinch for support. Our time together isn't over, and we look forward to continuing our fight to help families and children in our beloved Hyde Park community.

CHAPTER 43

CONCLUSION

The research and data I have gathered about poverty in America during the past sixty years has revealed that millions of poor Americans continue to struggle and battle poverty despite federal, state, and local program support and resources. The question is **why**?

In 2021, The Children's Defense Fund published a report on how to significantly reduce poverty in the US. The report is divided into ten modules. Each is titled with a different question and answers. I've decided to use the report and make personal comments accordingly. Each module is divided into paragraphs. It is my hope that the answers to the questions will help readers understand why poverty won't go away unless drastic changes are made at all government levels.[98]

Module 1 – What is poverty and how might we measure it? Characteristics include low income based on predetermined poverty line for individuals and families, lack of freedom politically and socially, belief in being disenfranchised, and socially excluded and deprived. The most logical and most reported poverty characteristic is not having enough money for families to live above the poverty line. However, characteristics not related to money may have more influence on the poor than is commonly thought. If you woke up every day and felt that you had no voice in political and social decisions, how would you feel? If you woke up every morning and felt that you were not included in the American dream; How would you feel? If you woke up every morning and felt that you were insignificant, how would you feel? The answer is walk in a poor person's shoes for a day!

Module 2 – Have you or someone you know experienced poverty? My brief exposure to situational poverty brought up questions that I had not felt before my father died and our family moved to the projects. I often felt guilty about our family's poverty. Was I to blame, Was I lazy? Have I made poor decisions? Is my attitude too negative? Did I have the work skills to help? Was I branded with a stigma? Was I a disgrace to my family? Did I lack motivation? Did I fail to work hard and put out enough effort? These hypotheticals are supposedly poverty myths. I am not quite so sure they are. A poor person goes through a series of questions looking for answers to why and tries to rationalize how to overcome these feelings, in many situations, especially the poor in generational poverty who never overcome these beliefs. It is not always about money!

Module 3 – What are the realities versus the myths of poverty? The American "safety net" is weak and filled with gaps and holes. The safety net is part of the overall federal budget. In 2019, 8 percent or $361 billion of the budget was devoted to individuals and families facing hardship. Safety net programs include: the refundable portions of the Earned Income Tax Credit; the Child Tax Credit, which assists low-and moderate-income working families; programs that provide cash payments to eligible individuals or households, including Supplemental Security Income (SSI) for the elderly or disabled poor and unemployment insurance; various forms of in-kind assistance for low-income people, including SNAP, low-income housing assistance, child care assistance, and help meeting home energy bills; and various other programs such as those that aid abused and neglected children.

In 2018, the safety net programs kept 37 million people out of poverty. Without the support poverty rate would have been 24.0 percent instead of 12.8 percent. Millions more with the support of these programs did not rise above the US poverty line.

Despite the number and variety of safety net programs, the US expends the fewest resources to get people out of poverty. It does not provide universal health care, affordable child care and low-income housing. Our poverty rate is twice that of some European countries and Canada with roughly the same Gross Domestic Product (GDP) . Because of economic and political failings that include welfare reforms and budget cuts, support has become weaker in the last 40 years.

Module 4 – What is the logic behind statistical probabilities? The probability of predicting poverty is based on demographic factors like age, race, gender, marital status, and education. Also, personal factors like the loss of a job, a health emergency, death in the family, families splitting up, can throw you into poverty. When these factors are analyzed over a fifteen-year period the possibility of falling into poverty increases.

Module 5 – Why are the five background factors so important...education, race, gender, marital status, and age. In general, those with less education, who are non-white, female, not married and in their 20s and 30s (or 60s or 70s) have higher odds of experiencing poverty than those with more education, who are white, male, married, and in their 40s and 50s.

Based on my personal experiences...the loss of my father and his income were strong contributors to our short-term poverty. We were fortunate to work our way out of poverty through a strong work ethic and the realization that we had lived in an environment that was not impoverished for more than 14 years. The institutionalized poverty mindset was not ingrained in our minds. We had hope!

Module 6 – How can we understand the root causes of poverty? The answer to this question begins with the facts that there are not enough viable opportunities for all Americans, inability of economic and political structures to provide supports to lift all Americans out of poverty, and mismatch of decent paying jobs versus the pool of labor in search of jobs.

In the past 40 years, the US economy has been producing more and more low-paying jobs, part-time jobs, and jobs that lack benefits. Social policies have been ineffective in reducing poverty. To combat the labor issue hourly wages need to be increased, programs that upgrade job skills and and provide new training are needed to offset inflation and the cost of living.

I agree with the root causes of poverty and the specifics related to jobs, however, there just might be a bell curve factor that should be considered. The bell curve concept has a relationship to the normal distribution. The term bell curve originates from the fact that the graph used to depict a normal distribution consists of a symmetrical bell-shaped curve. The highest point on the curve, or top of the bell, represents the most probable event in a series of data, while other possible occurrences are symmetrically distributed around the mean, creating a downward-sloping curve on each side of the peak. [99]

The bell curve is a graph depicting the normal distribution, which has a shape of a bell. To illustrate poverty, the mean, or center, of the curve corresponds with a majority of the population. On the right side of the curve the population decreases to people with high wealth (rich). The left side of the curve corresponds with the population that decreases to people with low wealth (poor). The basic subject of the bell curve is what should be done to help the poor. It is my belief that regardless of an increase in social programs or policies there will always exist a low percentage of the population that will remain poor (with various reasons for being poor) and there will always be a low percentage of the population that will be rich. Thus the middle class is at the peak with declining income on the left and right sides of the bell.

I hesitate to use the bell curve because of its link to race, intelligence and class structure. Despite the controversy, I believe the normal distribution theory applies to poverty.

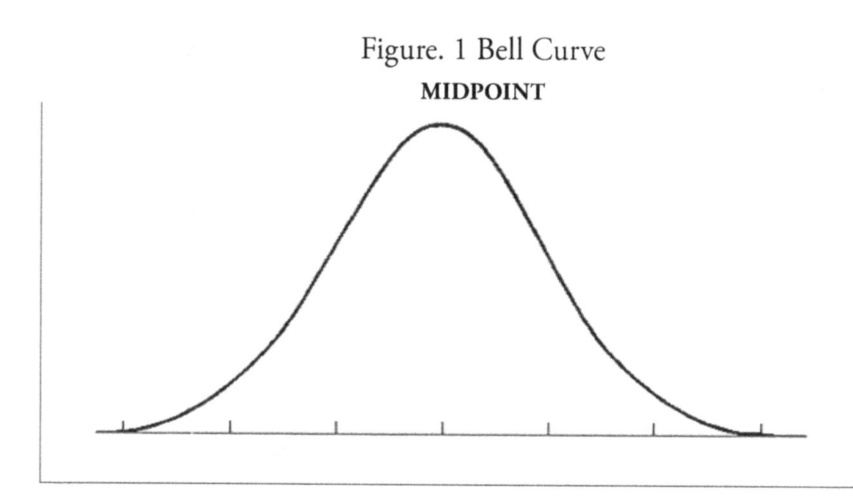

Figure. 1 Bell Curve

POVERTY WEALTH

Module 7 – How important is hard work and effort for avoiding poverty. Both are important but they do not always guarantee success. Many may still may not be able to get ahead economically because of factors mentioned previously like...poor physical/mental health, education, age, race, etc. How important is motivation...internal self-motivation/external motivation and determination for avoiding poverty. In Chapter 9, I discussed the nature versus nurture concept...behavioral and personality characteristic influenced by nature (environment) or nurture defined by genetics/DNA. Theorists have supported one or the other or a combination of the concepts over time. The probability that each influence who we are is more likely.

Which brings me back to the question of motivation and determination to avoid poverty. I believe that both could be influenced internally or externally. We may be born with the characteristic or be influenced by the environment (parents, peers, teachers, etc.).

Module 8 – Why is poverty higher in the US ? In 2019, Organization for Economic Cooperation and Development (OECD) data found that the US rate of poverty is substantially higher and more extreme than those found in 25 nations. The US has far and away the highest rate of poverty in developed countries. The US was ranked fourth at 17.8 percent, South Africa at 26.6 percent, Costa Rica at 20.9 percent and Romania 17.9 percent. The average poverty rate for the 25 countries was 10.7 percent. [100]

When the US poverty rate is compared with Canadian and European countries it is higher. The 2020 Canadian poverty rate was 11.27 percent…720 million Canadian dollars spent per year and the 2018 European average poverty rate was 9.8… 606 billion euros spent per year or 26.7 percent. In 2018, the poverty rate in America was 13.7 percent. [101]

The US poverty rate continues to remain high because there is little coordination and no master plan in 50 years. The current system is centered on in-kind benefits (food stamps, housing vouchers, heating subsidies) as opposed to cash, and has resulted in failed policies and programs. The US devotes little of its resources to combat poverty because of a lack of political influence by a change in presidents and Congressional party control. The US safety net (earned income tax credit, child tax credit, SSI, SNAP) is much weaker than peer countries. [102]

When poverty is high there is a failure to institutionalize equality, by providing a wide range of social insurance programs that prevent families from falling into poverty. Included are family and children allowance with cash assistance, far more generous unemployment assistance, universal health care, childcare, and more government income support.

The impact of COVID – 19 on the poverty rate shows the need for governmental support. There was a big drop in the American poverty rate during the pandemic. In 2018, the poverty rate was 13.9 percent. In 2021 the poverty rate was 7.7 percent. Why? SNAP increases, stimulus checks (cash not in-kind), housing evictions were barred, safety net programs were increased and government policies were changed. [103]

The dramatic difference between the poverty rate before COVID – 19 is noteworthy. It is quite obvious that cash payments rather than in-kind support are more beneficial to poor families and instrumental in decreasing the poverty rate. Why can't some Congressional leaders accept this option and do the right thing for poor families? When considering the overall benefit of reducing poverty, it will put more people back to work, stimulate the economy and increase the tax base...LOGIC..." pay now or pay later."

Module 9 - Why is it important to reduce poverty? The correlation between health and poverty is obvious. A person's health is negatively affected by lower economic status, particularly impoverishment. Poverty is associated with a host of health risks, including heart disease, diabetes, hypertension, cancer, infant mortality, mental illness, undernutrition, lead poisoning, asthma, dental problems, obesity, and a short life expectancy. Poverty further influences an increase in crime, addiction, incarceration, and child abuse. The outcome...the general public ends up paying a heavy price for allowing poverty.

Module 10 - What can be done to alleviate poverty? Reduce the poverty rate individually and as a nation. Create adequately paying jobs, raise the minimum wage, increase earned income tax credit, stimulate the creation of good quality jobs, improve housing conditions, improve health childcare, and create a strong and effective social network at national, state, and local levels.

I have completed a lot of research for this novel that directly relates to poverty. I firmly believe that presidential policies and programs have more impact on poverty than other factors. My research on presidential policies and programs over the past forty years has led me to believe that our governmental system has failed people in poverty. Presidential and Congressional party changes have resulted in abandoning good policies and programs that work. A good example is President Obama's Affordable Care Act. It has helped millions of poor people, yet when President Trump was elected to office, his first measure was to replace and repeal the Act. The attempt was also supported by the Senate majority. Fortunately, the Supreme Court ruled that it was not unconstitutional, and the Act was upheld. My point...if a policy or program works, don't get rid of it. All too often that is the case, and the poor never get ahead. "I have a dream."

My final comment and opinion...generational poverty has become institutionalized in America. Millions of individuals and families tend to give up, lose their will, become defeated, feel beaten and discard hope. The loss of self-confidence and the desire to aspire frequently becomes the major poverty issue, not money.

In the Introduction, I wrote that this novel was my first, and that I had to research how to construct a story that included essential writing components like a good idea, timeline, writing principles, and literary devices. I am comfortable that these practices were achieved.

Research led to an article about "secrets" to write a better story. Secrets included ensuring a good dialogue, creating suspense, portraying drama, and knowing the rules and breaking them. I hope that my attempt at adhering to these secrets was fulfilled. I am not sure I knew all of the rules, but I am sure I broke a number of them.

My original idea centered on writing a novel that would inspire readers to work hard and expend a lot of effort to achieve the proverbial "American Dream." I believe that I achieved that goal but recognized that poverty was a significant impediment to reaching it. I believe that my personal exposure to situational poverty influenced the educational path I chose and the career that I selected. Political realities help me realize that poor people are America's greatest challenge, and poverty will continue to exist unless significant changes are made in our political system.

Interlude Five

I turned the knob on the front door of our home and entered. I was greeted warmly by Latisha. "How was your work at the clinic today," she asked? "All went well," I said. I shared some of my progress with her. "We helped thirteen families with immediate food, nutrition, and resource support. Our volunteers are tremendous! Tomorrow, we will offer outreach support to three community centers. Our work is well received, and the University is extremely supportive. The clinic has become a tremendous asset to the community."

"How's your research on community needs going?" Latisha inquired. I responded, "The KIDS Count data has provided invaluable data about the communities' race/ethnic population, income and poverty rates. We use the information to determine the number of families and children that need support, resources and services." Latisha responded, "Sounds like your team is having an impact on helping a lot of poor people."

"Did you finish your research on presidents and poverty?" Latisha asked. "Yes, I did, and I traced the policies and programs of ten presidents from John Kennedy to George W. Bush. Each president was concerned with poverty and enacted a number of laws...some helped some did not. There were always influences like a change in presidents, congressional veto, constituent disapproval and more. The list goes on and on. I finally concluded that the presidential attempts toward solving the poverty problem was never ending. I am not sure poverty will ever be erased from our country."

I explained, "My chapter on Donald Trump was disheartening. Not that he wasn't concerned or didn't want to help the poor, but his attitude toward so many things was appalling." I continued to share my opinions about Trump and his policies to help the rich get richer,

Trump's programs and policies toward decreasing or changing legislation that helped the poor were significant. His attempt to repeal and replace the Affordable Care Act was disturbing. The ACA had become a health miracle for millions and millions of Americans that did not have health insurance. The most notable negative of his presidency was the encouragement and support that he gave the domestic terrorists who attacked Congress on January

6th. I was never so outraged and shocked at a president's behavior during my life. I will never forget that infamous day as long as I live.

Trump's denial and lack of concern for those Americans that contracted or died from COVID – 19 was apprehensible. An American president that did not encourage basic prevention strategies like wearing masks, social distancing and washing your hands does not have compassion. He never demonstrated positive feelings for the millions who suffered and for the thousands who became sick. Because of Trump's unpopular policies and decisions millions of Americans became disappointed with his presidency.

As you know, President Biden followed Trump and it was his responsibility to pick up the broken pieces. He took responsibility for the pandemic and ushered through resources for hospitals, health care facilities, state and local governments and expedited the inoculation of millions of Americans. His physical and human infrastructure efforts are underway. I await their outcome.

As I approached the concluding chapter, I added one more chapter on Equity and Equality. I told Latisha that the concepts were so important to poverty that I had to write about them. In my research I concluded that all Americans deserve a full and healthy life. *Equality* aims to ensure that everyone gets the same things in order to enjoy life. "Unfortunately, not everyone achieves that goal for various rcasons," I said. I told Latisha that federal, state, and local governments must be just, impartial, and fair for equity to be realized by millions of poor people.

"Is that the final chapter, Latisha asked?" "Yes, and I 'll prepare you now, it has a couple of bold and opinionated statements that will not be appreciated by some of my readers." Latisha commented, "Well, they don't have to read it then." I opened the door and walked onto the porch The screen door closed with a bang. I sat back on my rocking chair and rocked a little and thought about my final chapter A few minutes later Latisha spoke from the screen door and said, "Wow, that was some tirade. Looks like you exhausted yourself with that exposé, let's go out for supper tonight. It's almost eight o'clock, and I am not in the mood to cook," Latisha spoke. I said, "That's a great idea, and I promise to leave "Follow Me" at home.

EPILOGUE

I had taken my customary seat on the rocking chair on a cool and clear summer evening. A recent downpour had cooled things after a week of ninety-degree temperature. As I rocked, I gazed up and down the street. I noticed a familiar face approaching our house with skateboard reeling. When he got to the front of our house, he jumped off the board and flipped it into his awaiting hands. Pretty impressive, I thought. I immediately rose to my feet to greet him. "Hi, I haven't seen you in a few months," I said. "Yaa, I broke my leg skateboarding, and this is my first day back." "Sorry to hear that," I responded. "Would you like some water or soda," I asked. "Yes, he spoke eagerly."

I didn't know the boy's name, but he looked familiar, and I was certain I had seen him previously. "What's your name? "I asked. "My real name is James Matthews, and I was named after my father and grandfather. My friends and family call me "Jimmy," he spoke. "I need to ask you something that's very important to me," I spoke. "What is it?" Jimmy asked. "Have we ever met, and did I begin telling you a story about my life a few months ago?" I questioned. "Yes, a few months ago, you started telling me a story, but you fell asleep, so I left." Jimmy responded.

At that moment, Latisha walked on to the porch…door slamming as she approached us. "Who's your friend?" she asked. "His real name is James, but he likes to be called "Jimmy," Louis said. "Happy to meet you." Latisha said. Louis excitedly told Latisha that Jimmy was the young boy whom he began telling his story to a few months ago. "He hasn't been around because he broke his leg," Louis spoke. "You mean that dream you had about telling your life story to a young boy was true?" she asked. "Yes, it was real, and Jimmy can attest to it." Latisha asked, "You're saying that it wasn't a dream?" "Yes, I said, it was real."

Jimmy listened intently, and finally asked, "Do you think I could have that water now?" I said "Certainly." I asked Latisha to get Jimmy some water. Within minutes the door slammed, and Jimmy was guzzling down the water. He finished his drink with a burp and said, "Excuse me." He looked at Latisha and me and said, "Got to go, time for supper." Will we see you again, I asked?" He responded, "How about tomorrow, Louis. I would like to hear more of your story." "Great, see you tomorrow "I responded.

Latisha sat down next to me dismayed. "I can't believe that you actually were telling your story to a real person. I always thought that it was a dream or a figment of your imagination. That experience led to you writing your life's story, because of a little boy's surprise visit and desire to listen to you. I guess he may not be the only one who learns about your life," she spoke. I responded, "There may be thousands of people waiting to "Follow Me."

My story has ended. I hope you have enjoyed my journey and have "followed me" through seventy years of my life. Since my early years until this day, I have always felt a kindred spirit for the poor, especially during and after my exposure to situational poverty. As I matured and gained more direct experience through internships, on the job training and fieldwork my passion and resolve continued to evolve and grow. I have become more sensitive to the hardships of poor families and children than I had expected. I plan on continuing my quest for answers and solutions to poverty.

I have given much thought to my next book. I have decided to continue my story with the continued emphasis on poverty. I plan on documenting Biden's presidency from month to month and supporting my information with quantifiable and qualitative data. My quest has begun…Follow Me - 2022!

POST PREFACE

When I decided to write a fictional novel about a teen growing up in a large city, I researched a number of options. I wanted to write a story about a teeen influenced by poverty, cultural experiences and historical events that occurred during his life.

The outcome…I chose the Chicago southside. The two areas I chose had a number of differences…crime rates, poverty levels, educational resources and services and children and family supports. Two areas were selected Hyde Park and Fuller Park. Both were largely populated with African Americans. Hyde Park had less strife, crime and was considered more affluent.

I lived in each area growing up and was influenced by the differences between both. I drew on both areas to shape and mold my beliefs and career goals.

While writing, I decided to use real places like…the University of Chicago, Chicago Child Care Society, Chicago Food Depository and local high schools. Characters' names are fictional and chosen randomly. Historical events, presidential policies/programs and data/statistics are real and developed according to a timeline.

As I matured, my life experiences, work and education contributed to my knowledge base and career choices and are reflected in the novel.

Multiple sources were used to provide credibility and accuracy to the story. I referenced a number of books and articles to assure readers that poverty has existed for generations and an important political and social concern of mine during my life.

CHARTS/FIGURE

Page

SOURCES

Part I:

Chapter 2: Early Years

NO. **Page**

1. *"10 Secrets to Write Better Stories"* Bunting, Joe. · 3
2. "Four Basic Principles in Writing Fiction" ritingcommons.org, Welker H. Riley · · 10
3. *"Essential Literary Devices and How to Use Them in Your Writing"* www.masterclass.com. · 10
4. *"1959 Chicago White Sox"* sabr.org · 14
5. "*Cuban Missile Crisis*" www.historty.com · 15
6. "*The Presidents and the Poor America Battles Poverty: 1964-2017*" McAndrews, Lawrence, J. 2018, University Press of Kansas. · · · · · · · · · · · · · · · · 17
7. Ibid. · 17
8. "Chicago Public School Boycott, www.facinghistory.org · 20
9. "List of American Music of 1960" www.thepeoplehistor.com · · · · · · · · · · · · · · · · 21
10. "List of American Films of 1960" m.imb.com · 22
11. "Midnight Flight" suburbanchicagoland.com, Hanania, Ray · · · · · · · · · · · · · · · 26
12. *"Chicago Gangs"* www.history.com. · 30
13. "*Gangs in Chicago*" www.encyclopedia. www.changehistory.org · · · · · · · · · · · · · 31

Part II:

Chapter 4: Cultural Influences

14. "*How the Hippie Movement Influenced the VietNam War*" www.history.com Pruitt, Sarah · 34
15. "*History of the Hippie Movement*" www.britannica.com · 34

16. "*Civil Rights Act*" www.history.com · 35
17. "*Chicago Freedom Movement*" www.blackpadst.org · 36
18. "*Assassination of Martin Luther King Jr.*" kinginstitute.stanford.edu · · · · · · · · · · · 37
19. "*Fair Housing act – History*" www.history.com · 38
20. "*Chicago Seven*" www.smithsonianmag.com · 38
21. "*One Great Leap for Mankind*" www.nasa.com · 39
22. "*President Nixon*" www.whitehouse.gov · 40
23. "Voting Rights Act" www.ourdocuments.gov · 40
24. "*Richard Nixon 37th US President*" www.britannica.com · · · · · · · · · · · · · · · · · · 40

Chapter 9: Nurture versus Nature
25. "Genes or Environment?" www.verywellmind.com · 71

Part III:
Chapter 15: Presidential Election - 1976
26. "Presidential Campaign:1976" www.britannica.com · 98
27. "*The Presidents and the Poor America Battles Poverty: 1964-2017*"
McAndrews, Lawrence J, 2018, University Press of Kansas. · · · · · · · · · · · · · · · · 99

Chapter 18: Job Offer
28. ccc.society.com · 107

Chapter 23: Latisha
29. "Nervous Breakdown" healthgrades.com · 127

PART IV
Chapter 24: Research Proposal
30. "Child Care Society" www.cccsociety.org · 133
31. "Implementing Evidence-Based Social Work Practice"
Mullen, E. J., Bledsoe, S. E· 133
32. "Trends in Illinois Poverty Rates for Blacks and Hispanics" Simpson, Patricia · · 147
33. Ibid. · 148
34. "State Poverty Rates for Whites, Blacks and Hispanics in the late 1980's.
Javeman, Robert, Danziger, Sheldon, Plotnick, Robert, D. www.irpwisc.edu · · 149

35. "Illinois Poverty" www.uscensus.com 149
36. Ibid. 149
37. Ibid. 149
38. Ibid. 150

Chapter 30: September 11. 2001
39. "9/11" amp.cnn.com 157
40. "9/11" www.history.navy.military 157
41. "9/11" www.tsa.gov 158
42. "9/11" www.dhs.gov` 158

Chapter 31: Neighborhood Return
43. "The Incredible History and Cultural Legacy of the Bronzeville Neighborhood" chicagometropolisnewspaper.com, chicagotours.com 159
44. Ibid. 160
45. Ibid. 160

Part V:

Chapter 32: The Clinic
46. "Supplemental Nutrition Assistance Program (SNAP)" www.hhs.gov, www.sapling.com 171
47. "Women, Infants and Children (WIC)" www.hhs.gov, www.sapling.com 171
48. "Temporary Assistance for Needy Families (TANF)" www.hhs.gov, www.sapling.com 172
49. "Program History/Medicaid" www.medicaid.gov 172
50. "Children's Health Insurance Program" (CHIP) www.macpac.gov 172
51. "HUD" www.hhs.gov, www.sapling.com 172
52. "LIHEAP" www.hhs.gov, www.sapling.com 172
53. "Aid to Families with Dependent Children (AFDC)" www.hhs.gov, www.sapling.com 172
54. "Supplemental Social Security (SSI)" www.usa. 172

Chapter 33: Food and Nutrition
55. "Chicago Food Depository" www.chicagofoodbank.org 175

Chapter 34: KIDS Count
56. "Casey Foundation" www.act.org, www.datacenter kidscount.org, www.aecf.org 178
57. "Kids Count" www.voiceforkids.org. Bryant, Bill 179
58. Ibid. 179
59. Ibid. 179

Chapter 35: Presidents and Poverty
60. "LBJ" whitehouse.gov 181
61. Richard Nixon: *"The Presidents and the Poor America Battles"Poverty: 1964-2017*: McAndrews, Lawrence J, 2018, University Press of Kansas. 183
62. "Gerald Ford, *"The Presidents and the Poor America Battles Poverty"* www.pbr.org 183
63. Ibid. 184
64. "Jimmy Carter'" www.whitehouse.gov, www.presidency.uscb.edu 185
65. "Ronald Reagan" quizlet.com, pubmed.ncbi.nim.nih.gov 186
66. "George H.W. Bush" millercenter.com 186
67. "Bill Clinton" clinton whitehouse archives.gov, www.jstor.org 187
68. "George W. Bush" millercenter.org, files.eric.gov, NCLB An Anti-poverty Measure, vittana.org. Gaille, Louise. 188
69. "Barack Obama – Key Events" millercenter.org 189
70. "The Pros and Cons of Obamacare" www.healthline.com 189
71. "Who Will the Affordable Care Act Benefit the Most?" www.buffalo.edu 189

Chapter 37: Donald J.Trump
72. "What Did Trump Inherit from Obama?" www.nbcnews.com, Chinni, Dante ·197
73. "United States Presidential Election of 2016" www.britannica.com, Beckwith, David 198
74. "Why Hillary Clinton Lost" amp.theatlantic.com, Ball, Molly November 15, 2016 198
75. "How America Became Poor Under Donald Trump, as Joe Biden Claims?" www.atlantic.com 200
76. Ibid. 200

77. "Trump Is Trying Hard to Thwart Obamacare, How's That Going?" Duffin-Simmons, Selena www.commonwealthfund.org 201

Chapter 38: COVID - 19
78. "A Timeline of COVID -19 Developments" www.ajmc.com, AJMC Staff, January 1, 2020/2021 203
79. "COVID Left Millions of Families Struggling" www.aecf.org 203
80. "COVID – 19 www.cdc.gov, theguardian.com 204
81. "All the President's Lies About the Coronavirus" www.theatlantic.com, Paz, Christian 205

Chapter 39: Joe Biden
82. "Biden's First 100 Days: Here's What to Expect" npr.org. Moore, Elena November 2020. 206
83. Ibid. 206
84. Ibid. 207
85. "Supreme Court Upholds Obamacare in 7-2 Ruling", Kruzel, John. "What Is so Special About the U.S. President's First 100 Days" www.voanews.com 207
86. "Biden Sells Human Infrastructure Plan Despite Imperiled Bipartisan Plan" www.usnews.com, "Health 208
87. "Healthcare" joebiden.com 208

Chapter 40: January 6, 2021
88. "Timeline of the 2001 United States Capital" www.washingtonpost.com 210

Chapter 41: Equity and Equality
89. "40 Ways Forward : Accountable Steps for a More Equitable America" Time, VOL, NOS. 19-20, 2021, Gajanan, Mahita. 212
90. "Enact Universal Healthcare" Time, VOL, 197, NOS. 19-20, 2021, Barkin, Andy 213
91. "Reform the Thrifty Food Plan" Time, VOL, 197, NOS. 19-20, 2021, Gilkesson, Parker, L. 213
92. "Integrate Schools" Time, VOL, 197, NOS. 19-20, 2021, Rooks, Nolliwe 214

CPSIA information can be obtained
at www.ICGtesting.com
Printed in the USA
LVHW041450300322
714839LV00015B/701

9 781638 373889